Griffin's
Easy to Pronounce
Italian

by
Cliff Davis

Griffin Publishing
Glendale, California

10 9 8 7 6 5 4 3 2 1

ISBN 1-882180-34-8

Griffin Publishing
544 Colorado Street
Glendale, California 91204

Telephone: 1-800-423-5789

Manufactured in the United States of America

INTRODUCTION

The EASY TO PRONOUNCE phrase book series has been developed with the conviction that learning to speak a foreign language should be fun and easy.

The EPLS Vowel Symbol System™ is a revolutionary phonetic tool which stresses consistency, clarity and above all, simplicity! The basic vowel symbols have been placed on the back cover for easy reference.

You will be amazed at how confidence in your pronunciation will lead to an eagerness to talk to other people in their own language.

Other Easy to Pronounce phrasebooks:

EASY TO PRONUNCE SPANISH
EASY TO PRONOUNCE FRENCH
EASY TO PRONOUNCE GERMAN
EASY TO PRONOUNCE JAPANESE

ACKNOWLEDGMENTS

Series Editor
Richard D. Burns, Ph.D.

Associate Series Editor
Mark M. Dodge, M.A.

President, EPLS Training
Betty Chapman, President

Research and Computer Imput
Pirscilla Leal Bailey

Italian Language Consulting Editor
Adriano Comollo

Coordinating Foreign Language Editor
Lorena Richins M.

Book Design and Typeset
Regina Books, Claremont, California

Cover Design
Sylvia Hoffland, Long Beach, California

Reviewers of Italian
Gitta Komenyi
Richard Collins

CONTENTS

PRONUNCIATION GUIDE

Most English speakers are familiar with the Italian word **Pizza**. This is how its correct pronunciation would be represented in this system.

PⒺⒺ´-TSⒶⓗ

All Italian vowel sounds are assigned a specific non changing symbol. When these symbols are used in conjunction with consonants and read normally, pronunciation of even the most difficult foreign word becomes incredibly EASY.

On the following page you find all the symbols used in this book. They are EASY to LEARN since their sounds are familiar. Beneath each symbol are three English words which contain the sound of the symbol.

THE SAME BASIC SYMBOLS ARE USED IN ALL EASY TO PRONOUNCE PHRASE BOOKS!

EPLS VOWEL SYMBOLS

(A)

Ace
Bake
Safe

(EE)

See
Green
Feet

(O)

Oak
Cold
Phone

(oo)

Cool
Pool
Tool

(ĕ)

Red
Pet
Bed

(ah)

Rock
Hot
Off

(oy)

Boy
Toy
Joy

(ow)

Cow
How
Now

EPLS CONSONANTS

Consonants are letters like **T**, **D**, and **K**. They are easy to recognize and their pronunciation seldom changes. The following pronunciation guide letters represent some unique Italian consonant sounds.

Ʀ	represents a slightly rolled r sound
Ʀ	represents a strongly rolled r sound
TS	represents the letter **z** in Italian. Pronounce the word hi**ts** without the **hi** or simply say pi**zz**a!
KY	pronounce like the **c** in **c**ute
CH	pronounce like the **ch** in **ch**air

PRONUNCIATION TIPS

- Each pronunciation guide word is broken into syllables. Read each word slowly, one syllable at a time, increasing speed as you become more familiar with the system.

- In Italian it is important to emphasize certain syllables. This mark (') over the syllable reminds you to stress that syllable.

- Most symbols are pronounced the way they look!

- Pronunciation and word choices in this book were chosen for their simplicity and effectiveness.

- Throughout the book you will see the abbreviation **PPC**. This stands for **per piacere** which means please in Italian. (**Per favore** also means please)

ESSENTIAL WORDS AND PHRASES

Here are some basic words and phrases that will help you express your needs and feelings in Italian.

Hello

Ciao

CH**ow**

How are you?

Come sta?

KÓ-M**A** ST**ah**

Fine/ Very well

Molto bene

MÓL-T**O** B**A**-N**A**

And you?

E lei?

ĕ L**A**-**EE**

Goodbye

Arrivederci

ah-R**EE**-V**A**-D**ĕ**R-CH**EE**

Good morning

Buon giorno

BWON JOR-NO

Good evening

Buona sera

BWO-Nah SE-Rah

Good night

Buona notte

BWO-Nah NOT-TA

Mr.

Signor

SEN-YOR

Mrs.

Signora

SEN-YO-Rah

Miss

Signorina

SEN-YO-REE-Nah

Yes

Sí

SEE

No

No

NO

Please

Per piacere / Per favore

PeR PEE-ah-CHA-RA

PeR Fah-VO-RA

Always remember to say **please** and **thank you**.

Thank you

Grazie

GRah-TSEE-A

Excuse me

Mi scusi

MEE SKOO-ZEE

I'm sorry

Mi dispiace

MEE DEES-PEE-ah-CHA

I'm a tourist

Sono un turista

SŌ-NŌ ŌON TŌO-RĒE'S-Tah

I don't speak Italian

Non parlo Italiano

NŌN Pah'R-LŌ ĒE-Tah-LĒE-ah'-NŌ

I speak a little Italian

Parlo un poco l'Italiano

Pah'R-LŌ ŌON PŌ'-KŌ
LĒE-Tah-LĒE-ah'-NŌ

Do you understand English?

Capisce l'inglese?

Kah-PĒE'-SHA LĒEN-GLA'-SA

I don't understand!

Non capisco!

NŌN Kah-PĒE'S-KŌ

Please repeat

Ripeta per favore

RĒE-PA'-Tah PĕR Fah-VŌ'-RA

I want...
Voglio ..

VÓL-YO...

I have...
Ho...

O...

I know
Lo so

LO SO

I don't know
Non lo so

NON LO SO

I like it
Mi piace

MEE PEE-ah-CHA

I don't like it
Non mi piace

NON MEE PEE-ah-CHA

I'm lost

Mi sono perduto (perduta for a female)

MⒺⒺ SⓄ-NⓄ PⒺR-DⓄⓄ-TⓄ (ah)

I'm in a hurry

Ho fretta

Ⓞ FRⒶT-Tah

I'm tired

Sono stanco (stanca for a female)

SⓄ-NⓄ STahN-KⓄ (ah)

I'm ill

Sono ammalato (ammalata for a female)

SⓄ-NⓄ ahM-Mah-Lah-TⓄ (ah)

I'm hungry

Ho fame

Ⓞ Fah-MⒶ

I'm thirsty

Ho sete

Ⓞ SⒶ-TⒶ

I'm angry

Sono adirato

SⓄ-NⓄ ah-DⒺⒺ-Rah-TⓄ

My name is...

Mi chiamo...

MEE KEE-ah-MO...

What's your name?

Come si chiama?

KO-MA SEE KEE-ah-Mah

Where are you from?

Di dov'è Lei?

DEE DO-VA LA-EE

Do you live here?

Lei abita qui?

LA-EE ah-BEE-Tah KWEE

I just arrived

Sono appena arrivato (a)

SO-NO ahP-PA-Nah ah-BEE-Vah-TO

What hotel are you [staying] at?

In quale hotel sta?

EEN KWah-LA O-TeL STah

I'm at the...hotel

Sono all' hotel...

SO-NO ahL O-TeL....

It was nice to meet you

E' stato un piacere incontrarla

Ⓐ STⓐ-TⓄ ㏄N PⒺ-ⓐ-CHⒶ-ⓇⒶ
ⒺN-KⓄN-TⓇⓐR-Lⓐ

See you next time

Arrivederci a presto

ⓐ-ⓇⒺ-VⒶ-DⓔR-CHⒺ ⓐ
PⓇⓔS-TⓄ

See you later

A più tardi

ⓐ PⒺ-㏄ Tⓐ R-DⒺ

So long!

Arrivederci

ⓐ-ⓇⒺ-VⒶ-DⓔR-CHⒺ

Good luck!

Buona fortuna!

BWⓄ-Nⓐ FⓄR-T㏄-Nⓐ

THE BIG QUESTIONS

Who?

Chi?

KⒺⒺ

Who is it?

Chi è?

KⒺⒺ   Ⓐ

What?

Cosa?

KⓄ́-Zⓐⓗ

What's that?

Che cos'è quello?

KⒶ   KⓄ́-ZⒶ   KWⓔ̈́L-LⓄ

When?

Quando?

KWⓐⓗ́N-DⓄ

Where?

Dove?

DⓄ́-VⒶ

Where is...?

Dov'è...?

DO-Vē...

Be sure to accent the second syllable!

Which?

Quale?

KW@h-L@

Why?

Perchè?

P@R-K@

How?

Come?

KO-M@

How much? (money)

Quanto costa?

KW@hN-TO   KOS-T@h

How long?

Per quanto tempo?

P@R   KW@hN-TO   T@M-PO

ASKING FOR THINGS

The following phrases are valuable when asking for directions, food or help, etc.

I would like...

Vorrei....

VO-RA...

I need...

Ho bisogno di...

O BEE-ZON-YO DEE...

Can you...

può...

PWO...

When asking for things be sure to say
please and thank you

Please	**Thank you**
Per piacere	Grazie
PER	GRah-TSEE-A
PEE-ah-CHA-RA	

PHRASEMAKER

Combine **I would like** with the following phrases beneath it and you will have a good idea how to ask for things.

I would like...

Vorrei....

---

more coffee

ancora del caffè

---

some water

dell' acqua

Dᴇ̃L Lᴀ̂ʜ-KWᴀʜ

---

some ice

del ghiaccio

Dᴇ̃L Gᴇᴇ-ᴀ̂ʜ-CHᴏ

---

the menu

Il menù

ᴇᴇL Mᴇ̃-Nᴏᴏ́

PHRASEMAKER

Here are a few sentences you can use when you feel the urge to say **I need**...or **can you**?

I need...

Ho bisogno...

 Ⓞ Bⓔⓔ-Z(Ⓞ)N-Y(Ⓞ)...

---

help

d'aiuto

D(ah)-Y(oo)-T(Ⓞ)

---

directions

di indicazioni

D(ⓔⓔ) (ⓔⓔ)N-D(ⓔⓔ)-K(ah)-TS(ⓔⓔ)-Ⓞ-N(ⓔⓔ)

---

more money

di più soldi

D(ⓔⓔ) P(ⓔⓔ)-(oo) S(Ⓞ)L-D(ⓔⓔ)

---

change

di moneta

D(ⓔⓔ) M(Ⓞ)-N(Ⓐ)-T(ah)

---

a lawyer

di un avvocato

D(ⓔⓔ) (oo)N (ah)V-V(Ⓞ)-K(ah)-T(Ⓞ)

Can you...

può...

PW①...

---

help me?

aiutarmi?

ⓐⓗ-Yⓞⓞ-Tⓐⓗ'R-Mⓔⓔ

---

show me?

indicarmi?

ⓔⓔN-Dⓔⓔ-Kⓐⓗ'R-Mⓔⓔ

---

give me...?

darmi...?

Dⓐⓗ'R-Mⓔⓔ

---

tell me...?

dirmi...?

Dⓔⓔ'R-Mⓔⓔ

---

take me to...?

portarmi al...?

Pⓞ®-Tⓐⓗ'R-Mⓔⓔ   ⓐⓗL...

ASKING THE WAY

No matter how independent you are, sooner or later you'll probably have to ask directions.

Where is...?

Dov'è?

DⓄ-Vⓔ́...

Is it near?

E' vicino?

Ⓐ Vⓔⓔ-CHⓔⓔ-NⓄ

Is it far?

E' lontano?

Ⓐ LⓄN-Tⓐⓗ́-NⓄ

I'm lost!

Mi sono perduto (perduta for a female)

Mⓔⓔ SⓄ́-NⓄ PⓔR-Dⓞⓞ́-TⓄ (ⓐⓗ)

I'm looking for...

Sto cercando...

STⓄ CHⓔR-KⓐⓗN-DⓄ...

PHRASEMAKER

Where is...

Dov'è...

DO-Vë...

---

the restroom?

la toilette?

L@ TW@-LëT

---

the telephone?

il telefono?

EL T@-L@-FO-NO

---

the beach?

la spiaggia?

L@ SPEE-@-J@

---

the hotel...?

l' hotel...?

LO-TëL

---

the train for...?

il treno per...?

EL TRë-NO PëR...

TIME

What time is it?

Che ora è?

K@   O'-R@   ê

Morning

Mattina

M@T-TEE'-N@

Noon

Mezzogiorno

M@-TS@-J@R-N@

Night

Notte

N@T-T@

Today

Oggi

@'-JEE

Tomorrow

Domani

D@-M@'-NEE

This week

Questa settimana

KWⒶS-TⓐⒽ SⒺT-TⒺⒺ-MⓐⒽ-NⓐⒽ

This month

Questo mese

KWⒶS-TⓄ MⒶ-SⒶ

This year

Questa' anno

KWⒶ-STⓐⒽ ⓐⒽN-NⓄ

Now

Adesso

ⓐⒽ-DⒺS-SⓄ

Soon

Presto

PRⒺS-TⓄ

Later

Più tardi

PⒺⒺ-ⓄⓄ TⓐⒽR-DⒺⒺ

Never

Mai

MⓐⒽ-ⒺⒺ

WHO IS IT?

I

Io

ⒺⒺ́-Ⓞ

You (Formal)   (Informal)

Lei   tu

LⒶ́-ⒺⒺ   TⓄⓄ

Use this form of you with   Use this form of you with
people you don't know well   people you know well

We

Noi

NⓄⓎ

They

loro

LⓄ́-RⓄ

THE, A (AN), AND SOME

To use the correct form of The, A (An), or Some, you must know if the French word is masculine or feminine. Often you will have to guess! If you make a mistake, you will still be understood.

The

il, lo, l'

ⒺL/LⓄ/L

The before a singular
masculine noun
(Il) man is handsome

i, gli

Ⓔ/LYⒺ

The before a plural
masculine noun
(I) men are handsome

La

LⓐⓗⒽ

The before a singular
feminine noun
(La) woman is pretty

i, le

Ⓔ/LⒶ

The before a plural
feminine noun
(I) women are pretty

A or An

un / uno

ⓄⓄN / ⓄⓄ-NⓄ

A or **an** before a
masculine noun
He is (un) man

una / un'

ⓄⓄN-ⓐⓗ / ⓄⓄN

A or **an** before a
feminine noun
She is (una) woman

Some

Qualche

KWⓐⓗL-KⒶ

Some before masculine and feminine nouns

USEFUL OPPOSITES

Near	**Far**
vicino	lontano
VEE-CHEE-NO	LON-Tah-NO

Here	**There**
Qui	Là
KWEE	Lah

Left	**Right**
Sinistra	Destra
SEE-NEES-TRah	DeS-TRah

A little	**A lot**
Un poco	Molto
ooN PO-KO	MOL-TO

More	**Less**
Di più	Meno
DEE PEE-oo	MA-NO

Big	**Small**
Grande	Piccolo
GRahN-DA	PEEK-KO-LO

Opened
Aperto
ⓐⓗ-Pⓔ́R-Tⓞ

Closed
Chiuso
KYⓞⓞ-Zⓞ

Cheap
A buon mercato
ⓐⓗ BWⓞN Mⓔ́R-Kⓐⓗ-Tⓞ Kⓐⓗ́-Rⓞ

Expensive
Caro

Clean
Pulito
Pⓞⓞ-Lⓔ́E-Tⓞ

Dirty
Sporco
SPⓞ́R-Kⓞ

Good
Buono
BWⓞ́-Nⓞ

Bad
Cattivo
KⓐⓗT-Tⓔ́E-Vⓞ

Vacant
Libero
Lⓔ́E-Bⓐ-Rⓞ

Occupied
Occupato
ⓞ-Kⓞⓞ-Pⓐⓗ́-Tⓞ

Right
Giusto
Jⓞⓞ́S-Tⓞ

Wrong
Sbagliato
SBⓐⓗL-Yⓐⓗ́-Tⓞ

WORDS OF ENDEARMENT

I love you

Ti amo

TEE ah-MO

My love

Amore mio

ah-MO-RA MEE-O

My life

Vita mia

VEE-Tah MEE-ah

My friend (to a male)

Amico mio

ah-MEE-KO MEE-O

My friend (to a female)

Amica mia

ah-MEE-Kah MEE-ah

Kiss me!

Baciami!

Bah-CHah-MEE

WORDS OF ANGER

What do you want?

Che cosa vuole?

KA KŌ´-Zah VWŌ-LA?

Leave me alone!

Mi lasci in pace!

MEE Lah´-SHEE EEN Pah´-CHA

Go away!

Vada via!

Vah´-Dah VEE´-ah

Stop bothering me!

Non mi stia a seccare!

NON MEE STEE´-ah ah SAK-Kah-RA

Be Quiet!

Silenzio!

SEE-LĒN-TSEE-O

That's enough!

Basta!

Bah´S-Tah

COMMON EXPRESSIONS

When you are at a loss for words but have the feeling you should say something, try one of these!

Who knows?

Chi lo sa?

KEE LO Sah

That's the truth!

E' la verità!

ĕ Lah Vĕ-REE-Tah

Sure!

Sicuro!

SEE-KOO-RO

Wow!

Che sorpresa!

KA SOR-PRA-Zah

What's happening?

Che cosa succede?

KA KO-Zah SOO-CHA-DA

I think so!

Penso di sí!

PAN-SO DEE SEE

Cheers!
Salute!
Sah-Loo-Ta

Good luck!
Buona fortuna!
BWO-Nah FOR-Too-Nah

With pleasure!
Con piacere!
KON PEE-ah-CHA-RA

My goodness!
Per l'amor del cielo!
PeR Lah-MOR DeL CHA-LO

What a shame or Thats too bad!
Peccato
PeK-Kah-TO

Well done! Bravo!
Bene! / Bravo!
BA-NA / BRah-VO

USEFUL COMMANDS

Stop!

Alt !

ⓐⱧLT

Go!

Forza!

FⓄR-TSⓐⱧ

Wait!

Aspetti!

ⓐⱧ-SPⒶT-TⒺⒺ

Hurry!

Ho fretta!

Ⓞ FRⒶT-TⓐⱧ

Slow down!

Rallenti!

RⓐⱧL-LⒺN-TⒺⒺ

Come here!

Venga qui!

VⒺN-GⓐⱧ KWⒺⒺ

Help!

Aiuto!

ⓐⱧ-Yⓞⓞ-TⓄ

EMERGENCIES

Fire!

Al fuoco!

@L FWO-KO

Emergency!

Emergenza!

E-MER-JEN-TSah

Call the police!

Chiamate la polizia!

KEE-ah-Mah-TA Lah PO-LEE-TSEE-ah

Call a doctor!

Chiamate un medico!

KEE-ah-Mah-TA OON MA-DEE-KO

Call an ambulance!

Chiamate un' ambulanza.!

KEE-ah-Mah-TA OON
ahM-BOO-Lah N-TSah

I need help

Ho bisogno d'aiuto

O BEE-ZON-YO Dah-YOO-TO

ARRIVAL

Passing through customs should be easy since there are usually agents available who speak English. You may be asked how long you intend to stay and if you have anything to declare.

- Have your passport ready.

- Be sure all documents are up to date.

- While in a foreign country, it is wise to keep receipts for everything you buy.

- Be aware that many countries will charge a departure tax when you leave. Your travel agent should be able to find out if this affects you.

- If you have connecting flights, be sure to reconfirm them in advance.

- Make sure your luggage is clearly marked inside and out.

- Take valuables and medicines in carry on bags.

SIGNS TO LOOK FOR:

DOGANA (CUSTOMS)

BAGAGLI (BAGGAGE)

KEY WORDS

Baggage
Bagaglio

B@h-G@hL-Y@

Customs
Dogana

D@-G@h-N@h

Documents
Documenti

D@-K@-M@N-T@

Passport
Passaporto

P@S-S@h-P@R-T@

Porter
Facchino

F@K-K@-N@

Tax
Imposta

@M-P@S-T@h

USEFUL PHRASES

I have nothing to declare

Non ho nulla da dichiarare

NON O NOOL-Lah Dah
DEE-KEE-ah-Rah-RA

I'll be staying...

Resterò qui...

↓ RES-TE-RO KWEE...

one week

una settimana

OO-Nah SET-TEE-Mah-NA

two weeks

due settimane

DOO-A SET-TEE-Mah-NA

one month

un mese

OON MA-SA

two months

due mesi

DOO-A MA-SEE

I'm here on business

Sono in viaggio d'affari

SŌ-NO EEN VEE-ah-JO DahF-Fah-REE

I'm here on vacation

Sono in vacanza

SŌ-NO EEN Vah-KahN-TSah

Here is my passport

Ecco (il mio) passaporto

ēK-KO EEL MEE-O
PahS-Sah-PŌR-TO

Is there a problem?

Ci sono dei problemi?

CHEE SŌ-NO DĀ-EE
PRO-BLĀ-MEE

I don't understand

Non capisco!

NON Kah-PEES-KO

Do you speak English?

Parla l'inglese?

PahR-Lah LEEN-GLĀ-Zah

PHRASEMAKER

Where is...

Dov'è?

DⓄ-Vⓔ
́...

customs?

la dogana?

Lⓐⓗ DⓄ-Gⓐⓗ
́-Nⓐⓗ

baggage claim?

il ritiro bagagli?

ⒺⒺL RⒺⒺ-TⒺⒺ
́-RⓄ Bⓐⓗ-Gⓐⓗ
́L-YⒺⒺ

the money exchange?

l'ufficio di cambio?

LⓄⓄ-FⒺⒺ
́-CHⓄ DⒺⒺ KⓐⓗM-BⒺⒺ-Ⓞ

the taxi stand?

il posteggio dei taxi?

ⒺⒺL PⓄ-STⒶ
́-JⓄ DⒶ TⓐⓗK-SⒺⒺ

the bus stop?

la fermata dell' autobus?

Lⓐⓗ FⓔR-Mⓐⓗ
́-Tⓐⓗ DⓔL
LⓄⓦ
́-TⓄ-BⓄⓄS

I need a porter!

Ho bisogno di un facchino!

Ⓞ BⒺⒺ-ZⓄ'N-YⓄ DⒺⒺ ⓄⓄN FⓐⓗK-KⒺⒺ'-NⓄ

These are my bags

Queste sono le mie valige

KWⒶ'S-TⒶ SⓄ'-NⓄ LⒶ MⒺⒺ'-Ⓐ Vⓐⓗ-LⒺⒺ'-JⒶ

I'm missing a bag

Mi manca una valigia

MⒺⒺ MⓐⓗN-Kⓐⓗ ⓄⓄ'-Nⓐⓗ Vⓐⓗ-LⒺⒺ'-Jⓐⓗ

Take my bags to a taxi please

Per favore porti le mie valige al taxi

PⒺⓔR Fⓐⓗ-VⓄ'-RⒶ PⓄ'R-TⒺⒺ LⒶ MⒺⒺ'-Ⓐ Vⓐⓗ-LⒺⒺ'-JⒶ ⓐⓗL TⓐⓗK-SⒺⒺ

Thank you. This is for you

Grazie. Questo e´ per lei

GRⓐⓗ'-TSⒺⒺ-Ⓐ KWⒶ'S-TⓄ Ⓐ PⒺⓔR LⒶ'-ⒺⒺ

HOTEL SURVIVAL

A wide selection of accommodations, ranging from the most basic to the most extravagant, are available wherever you travel in Italy. When booking your room, find out what amenities are included for the price you pay.

- Make reservations well in advance and get written confirmation of reservation before you leave home.

- Always have identification ready when checking in.

- Hotels in some foreign countries may require you to hand over your passport when checking in. It is usually returned the next day.

- Do not leave valuables, prescriptions or cash in your room when you are not there!

- Electrical items like blow dryers may need an adaptor. Your hotel may be able to provide one, but to be safe take one with you.

KEY WORDS

Hotel

Hotel

Ⓞ-Tⓔ́L

Bellman

Fattorino

Fⓐ́T-TⓄ-Rⓔ́Ⓔ-NⓄ

Maid

cameriera

Kⓐ-MⒶ-Rⓔ́Ⓔ-Ⓐ́-Rⓐ

Message

Messaggio

MⓐS-Sⓐ́-JⓄ

Reservation

Prenotazione

PRⒶ-NⓄ-Tⓐ-TSⓔⓔ-Ⓞ́-Nⓐ

Room service

Servizio in camera

Sⓔ́R-Vⓔⓔ́-TSⓔⓔ-Ⓞ

ⓔⓔN Kⓐ́-Mⓐ-Rⓐ

CHECKING IN

My name is... (I am...)

Mi chiamo...

MEE KEE-ah-MO...

I have a reservation

Ho la prenotazione

O Lah PRA-NO-Tah-TSEE-O-NA

Have you any vacancies?

Avete stanze libere?

ah-VA-TA STah-N-TSA LEE-BA-RA

What is the charge per night?

Quanto costa per notte?

KWah-N-TO KOS-Tah
PER NOT-TA

Is there room service?

C'è il servizio in camera?

CHA EEL SeR-VEE-TSEE-O
EEN Kah-MA-Rah

PHRASEMAKER

I would like a room with...

Vorrei una stanza con...

V⊙-Ŕ④ ⊚́-N⒜
ST⒜́N-TS⒜ K⊙N...

a bath

un bagno

⊚N B⒜́N-Y⊙

a shower

una doccia

⊚́-N⒜ D⊙́-CH⒜

one bed

un letto

⊚N L⒠́T-T⊙

two beds

due letti

D⊚́-④ L⒠́T-T⒠

a view

la vista

L⒜ V⒠́S-T⒜

USEFUL PHRASES

Where is the dining room?

Dov'è la sala da pranzo?

DO-Vĕ́ Lah Sah-Lah Dah PRah̃N-TSO

Are meals included?

I pasti sono inclusi?

EE Pah́S-TEE SÓ-NO
EEN-KLoó-ZEE

What time is...

A che ora è...

↓ ah KA Ó-Rah A...

---

breakfast?

la colazione?

Lah KO-Lah-TSEE-Ó-NA

---

lunch?

il pranzo?

EEL PRah̃N-TSO

---

dinner?

la cena?

Lah CHÁ-Nah

My room key please

La chiave per piacere

L@ K©-@-V@ PPC

Are there any messages for me?

Ci sono dei messaggi per me?

CH© S©-N© D@ M@S-S@-J©
P©R M@

Please wake me at...

Per favore mi svegli alle...

↓ P©R F@-V©-R@ M©
SV©L-Y© @L-L@..

6:00	6:30
sei	sei e mezzo
S@-©	S@-© @ M@-TS©

7:00	7:30
sette	sette e mezzo
S@T-T@	S@T-T@ @ M@-TS©

8:00	8:30
otto	otto e mezzo
©T-T©	©T-T© @ M@-TS©

9:00	9:30
nove	nove e mezzo
N©-V@	N©-V@ @ M@-TS©

PHRASEMAKER

I need...

Ho bisogno...

 B(EE)-Z(O)N-Y(O)...

soap

di sapone

D(EE)   S(ah)-P(O)-N(A)

more towels

di altri asciugamani

D(EE)   (ah)L-TR(EE)   (ah)-SH(oo)-G(ah)-M(ah)-N(EE)

ice cubes

di cubetti di ghiaccio

D(EE)   K(oo)-B(A)T-T(EE)   D(EE)   G(EE)-(ah)-CH(O)

toilet paper

di carta igienica

D(EE)   K(ah)R-T(ah)   (EE)-J(A)-N(EE)-K(ah)

a bellman

di un fattorino

D(EE)   (oo)N   F(ah)T-T(O)-R(EE)-N(O)

a maid
di una cameriera

DEE ŌO'-Nah Kah-MA-REE-A'-Rah

the manager
del direttore

DĕL DEE-RAT-TŌ'-RA

a babysitter
di una babysitter

DEE ŌO'-Nah BA-BEE-SEE'-TĕR

an extra key
di una chiave extra

DEE ŌO'-Nah KEE-ah'-VA ĕKS-TRah

a hotel safe
di una cassaforte

DEE ŌO'-Nah Kah-Sah-FŌR-TA

clean sheets
lenzuola pulite

LĕN-TSWŌ'-Lah PŌO-LEE'-TA

more blankets
di altre coperte

DEE ah'L-TRA KŌ-PĕR-TA

PHRASEMAKER
(PROBLEMS)

There is no...

Manca...

M⒜N-K⒜...

hot water

l'acqua calda

L⒜-KW⒜   K⒜L-D⒜

heat

il riscaldamento

ⒺⒺL   ⒭ⒺⒺS-K⒜L-D⒜-MⒺ̃N-TⓄ

light

la luce

L⒜   LⓄⓄ-CHⒶ

electricity

la corrente

L⒜   KⓄ-Ⓡⓔ̃N-TⒶ

toilet paper

la carta igienica

L⒜   K⒜R-T⒜   ⒺⒺ-JⒶ-NⒺⒺ-K⒜

PHRASEMAKER
(SPECIAL NEEDS)

Do you have...

Avete...

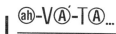

↓

facilities for the disabled?

accomodamenti per gli handicappati?

ⓐⓗ-KⓄ-MⓄ-Dⓐⓗ-Mⓔ́N-Tⓔⓔ Pⓔ̃R
LYⓔⓔ ⓐⓗN-Dⓔⓔ-KⓐⓗP-Pⓐⓗ́-Tⓔⓔ

a wheel chair?

una poltrona da invalido

ⓄⓄ́-Nⓐⓗ PⓄL-TRⓄ́-Nⓐⓗ
Dⓐⓗ ⓔⓔN-Vⓐⓗ-Lⓔⓔ́-DⓄ

an elevator?

un ascensore?

ⓄⓄN ⓐⓗ-SHⓐN-SⓄ́-Rⓐ

a ramp?

una rampa d'accesso?

ⓄⓄ́-Nⓐⓗ Rⓐⓗ́M-Pⓐⓗ Dⓐⓗ-CHⓐ́S-SⓄ

CHECKING OUT

The bill please

Vorrei il conto per piacere

VO-RA´ EEL KO´N-TO PPC

Is this bill correct?

Questo conto è esatto?

KWA´S-TO KO´N-TO A A-Zah´T-TO

Do you accept credit cards?

Accettate carte di credito?

ah-CHA-Tah´-TA Kah´R-TA
DEE KRA´-DEE-TO

Could you have my luggage brought down?

Potrebbe far portare giù le mie valige?

PO-TRA´B-BA FahR POR-Tah´-RA
Joo LA MEE´-A Vah-LEE´-JA

Can you call a taxi for me?

Potrebbe chiamarmi un taxi?

PO-TRA´B-BA KEE-ah-Mah´R-MEE
OON Tah´K-SEE

I had a very good time!

Ho passato dei giorni bellissimi!

Ⓞ Pⓐ͟hS-Sⓐ͟h′-TⓄ DⒶ JⓄ̈R-Nⓔⓔ Bⓔ̈L-Lⓔⓔ′S-Sⓔⓔ-Mⓔⓔ

Thanks for everything

Grazie di tutto

GRⓐ͟h′-TSⓔⓔ-Ⓐ Dⓔⓔ TⓞⓞT-TⓄ

I'll see you next time

Arrivederci a presto

ⓐ͟h-Rⓔⓔ-VⒶ-Dⓔ̈R-CHⓔⓔ ⓐ͟h PRⓔ̈S-TⓄ

Goodbye

Arrivederci

ⓐ͟h-Rⓔⓔ-VⒶ-Dⓔ̈R-CHⓔⓔ

RESTAURANT SURVIVAL

Italy is famous for its cuisine. You are encouraged to enjoy the vast array of regional specialties.

- Breakfast (la prima colazione) is usually served at your hotel. Lunch (il pranzo) is normally served from noon to 3:00 p.m., and dinner (la cena) from 7 p.m. to 10 p.m.

- Menus may contain the following statement; **servizio** (service charge). Note: A service charge is not a **mancia** (tip).

SIGNS TO LOOK FOR:

BAR OR SNACK BAR
TRATTORIA (LOCAL DISHES)
PIZZERIA (PIZZA PARLOR)
RISTORANTE (FINE DINNING)

KEY WORDS

Breakfast
Colazione

KO-L@h-TS@-O-N@

Lunch
Pranzo

PR@hN-TSO

Dinner
Cena

CH@-N@h

Waiter
Cameriere

K@h-M@-R@-@-R@

Waitress
Cameriera

K@h-M@-R@-@-R@h

Restaurant
Ristorante

R@S-TO-R@hN-T@

USEFUL PHRASES

A table for...

Un tavolo per...

↓ⒶN TⓐⒽ-VⓄ-LⓄ PⒺR...

2	4	6
due	quattro	sei
DⓄⓄ-Ⓐ	KWⓐⒽT-TRⓄ	SⒶ-ⒺⒺ

The menu please

Il menù, per piacere

ⒺⒺL MⒺ-NⓄⓄ PPC

Separate checks please

Conti separati, per piacere

KⓄN-TⒺⒺ SⒺ-PⓐⒽ-RⓐⒽ-TⒺⒺ PPC

We are in a hurry

Siamo di fretta

SⒺⒺ-ⓐⒽ-MⓄ DⒺⒺ FRⒶT-TⓐⒽ

What do you recommend?

Che cosa consiglia?

KⒶ KⓄ-ZⓐⒽ KⓄN-SⒺⒺL-YⓐⒽ

Prease bring me...

Per favore, mi porti...

PẼR FÂH-VÔ-RÂ MĒ PÔR-TĒ

Please bring us...

Per favore ci porti...

PẼR FÂH-VÔ-RÂ CHĒ PÔR-TĒ

I'm hungry

Ho fame

Ô FÂH-MÂ

I'm thirsty

Ho sete

Ô SÂ-TÂ

Is service included?

Il servizio é incluso?

ĒL SẼR-VĒ-TSĒ-Ô Â ĒN-KLŌ-ZÔ

The bill please

Vorrei il conto per piacere

VÔ-RÂ ĒL KÔN-TÔ PPC

ORDERING BEVERAGES

Ordering beverages is easy and a great way to practice your Italian! In many foreign countries you will have to request ice with your drinks.

Please bring me...

Per favore, mi porti...

PＥR Fah-VO-Ｂ A MＥE POR-TＥE...

---

coffee...

del caffè...

DＥL Kah-FA

tea...

del tè...

DＥL TA

---

with cream

con panna

KON Pah N-Nah

---

with sugar

con zucchero

KON TSoo-KA-Ｂ O

---

with lemon

con limone

KON LEE-MO-NA

---

with ice

con ghiaccio

KON GEE-ah-CHO

Soft drinks

Bibite

BEE-BEE-TA

Milk

Latte

LAHT-TA

Hot chocolate

Cioccolata

CHOK-KO-LAH-Tah

Juice

Succo

SOOK-KO

Orange juice

Succo di arancia

SOOK-KO DEE ah-Rah'N-CHah

Ice water

Acqua con ghiaccio

ah-KWah KON GEE-ah-CHO

Mineral water

Acqua minerale

ah-KWah MEE-NA-Rah-LA

AT THE BAR

Bartender

Barista

B@h-R@ES-T@h

The wine list please

La lista dei vini, per piacere

L@h   L@ES-T@h   D@   V@E-N@E   PPC

Cocktail

Cocktail

K@K-T@L

On the rocks

Con ghiaccio

K@N   G@E-@h-CH@

Straight

Senza ghiaccio

S@N-TS@h   G@E-@h-CH@

With lemon

con limone

K@N   L@E-M@-N@

PHRASEMAKER

I would like a glass of...

Vorrei un bicchiere di...

VO-RĀ́ ⓄN BEEK-Yḗ-RĀ DEE...

champagne

champagne

SHⓐM-PⓐÑ-Yⓐ

beer

birra

BEE-Rⓐ

wine

la lista dei vini, per piacere

Lⓐ LEE-Tⓐ DⒶ VEE-NEE PPC

red wine

vino rosso

VEE-NO ROS-SO

white wine

vino bianco

VEE-NO BEE-ⓐN-KO

ORDERING BREAKFAST

In Italy breakfast is usually small, consisting of caffelatte (coffee with milk) and bread, rolls or croissants.

Bread

Pane

Pah-NA

Toast

Pane tostato

Pah-NA TOS-Tah-TO

with butter

con burro

KON Boo-BO

with jam

con marmellata

KON Mah-MAL-L-ah-Tah

Cereal

Cereali

CHA-RA-ah-LEE

PHRASEMAKER

I would like...

Vorrei....

↓ VO-RA...

two eggs...

due uova...

DOO-A   WO-Vah...

with bacon

con pancetta

KON   Pah-N-CHAT-Tah

with ham

con prosciutto

KON   PRO-SHOOT-TO

with potatoes

con patate

KON   Pah-Tah-TA

HOW DO YOU WANT YOUR EGGS?

Scrambled / Fried

Strapazzate   Fritte

STRah-Pah-TSah-TA   FREET-TA

LUNCH AND DINNER

Although you are encouraged to sample great Italian cuisine, it is important to be able to order foods you are familiar with. This section will provide words and phrases to help you.

I would like...

Vorrei....

VO-RA...

We would like...

Vorremmo...

VO-RAM-MO...

Bring us...

Per favore ci porti...

PER Fah-VO-RA CHEE POR-TEE...

The lady would like...

La signora vorrebbe...

Lah SEEN-YO-Rah VO-RAB-BA...

The gentleman would like...

Il signore vorrebbe...

EEL SEEN-YO-RA VO-RAB-BA...

STARTERS

Appetizers
Antipasti

@N-T®-P@'S-T®

Bread and butter
Pane e burro

P@'-N@ @ B®-R®

Cheese
Formaggio

F®R-M@'-J®

Fruit
Frutta

FR®'T-T@

Salad
Insalata

®N-S@-L@'-T@

Soup
Minestra

M®-N@'S-TR@

MEATS

Beef

Manzo

M@N-TS©

Beef Steak

Bistecca

B€S-T@K-K@

Pork

Maiale

M@-Y@-L@

Ham

Prosciutto

PR©-SH©T-T©

Bacon

Pancetta

P@N-CH@T-T@

Lamb

Agnello

@N-Y€L-L©

Veal

Vitello

V€-T€L-L©

POULTRY

Baked chicken

Pollo al forno

POĹ-LO aL FOŔ-NO

Broiled chicken

Pollo alla griglia

POĹ-LO aĹ-Lah GREĹ-Yah

Fried chicken

Pollo fritto

POĹ-LO FREET-TO

Duck

Anitra

ah-NEE-TRah

Turkey

Tacchino

Tah-KEE-NO

Goose

Oca

O-Kah

SEAFOOD

Fish
Pesce
PⒶ-SHⒶ

Lobster
Aragosta
ⓐ-Rⓐ-GⓄS-Tⓐ

Oysters
Ostriche
ⓄS-TRⒺⒺ-Kⓐ

Salmon
Salmone
SⓐL-MⓄ-NⒶ

Shrimp
Gamberetti
GⓐM-BⒶ-RⒶT-TⒺⒺ

Trout
Trota
TRⓄ-Tⓐ

Tuna
Tonno
TⓄN-NⓄ

OTHER ENTREES

Sandwich
Panino

P(ah)-N(EE)-N(O)

Hot dog
Hot dog

(ah)T D(ah)G

Hamburger
Hamburger

(ah)M-B(oo)R-G(ĕ)R

French fries
Patatine fritte

P(ah)-T(ah)-T(EE)-N(A) FR(EE)T-T(A)

Pasta
Pasta

P(ah)S-T(ah)

Pizza
Pizza

P(EE)T-S(ah)

VEGETABLES

Carrots

Carote

Kah-RŌ-TA

Corn

Granturco

GRahN-TŌB-KŌ

Mushrooms

Funghi

FŌN-GEE

Onions

Cipolle

CHEE-PŌL-LA

Potato

Patate

Pah-Tah-TA

Rice

Riso

REE-ZŌ

Tomato

pomodoro

PŌ-MŌ-DŌ-BŌ

FRUITS

Apple
Mela
M@-L@

Banana
Banana
B@-N@-N@

Grapes
Uva
@-V@

Lemon
Limone
L@-M@-N@

Orange
Arancia
@-R@N-CH@

Strawberry
Fragola
FR@-G@-L@

Watermelon
Anguria
@N-G@-R@-@

DESSERT

Desserts
Dolci

DŌL-CH(EE)

Apple pie
Crostata di mela

KR(O)S-T(ah)́-T(ah) D(EE) M(A)́-L(ah)

Cherry pie
Crostata di ciliege

KR(O)S-T(ah)́-T(ah) D(EE) CH(EE)L-Y(A)́-J(A)

Pastries
Pasticcini

P(ah)S-T(EE)-CH(EE)́-N(EE)

Candy
Caramella

K(ah)-R(ah)-M(A)́L-L(ah)

Ice cream
Gelato

J(ĕ)-L(ah)́-T(O)

Ice cream cone

Cono di gelato

KÓ-NO DEE JĕL-Lah́-TO

Chocolate

Cioccolata

CHOK-KO-Lah́-Tah

Strawberry

Fragola

FRah́-GO-Lah

Vanilla

Vaniglia

Vah-NEEĹ-Yah

CONDIMENTS

Salt	**Pepper**
Sale	Pepe
S(ah)́-L(A)	P(A)́-P(A)

Sugar

zucchero

TS(oo)́-K(A)-R(O)

Mayonnaise

Maionese

M(ah)-Y(O)-N(A)́-S(A)

Butter

burro

B(oo)́-R(O)́

Mustard

Senape

S(A)́-N(ah)-P(A)

Ketchup

Ketchup

K(e)̆́-CH(oo)P

Vinegar and oil

Aceto e olio

(ah)-CH(A)́-T(O)   (A)   (O)́L-Y(O)

SETTINGS

A cup

Una tazza

A glass

Un bicchiere

A spoon

Un cucchiaio

A fork

Una forchetta

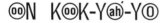

A knife

Un coltello

A plate

Un piatto

A napkin

Un tovagliolo

HOW DO YOU WANT IT COOKED?

Baked

Al forno

@L FO'R-N@

Roasted

Arrosto

@-R@'S-T@

Steamed

Al vapore

@L V@-P@'-R@

Fried

Fritte

FR@'T-T@

Rare

Al sangue

@L S@N-GW@

Medium

Cotta normale

KO'T-T@ N@R-M@'-L@

Well done

Ben cotta

B@N KO'T-T@

PROBLEMS

I didn't order this

Non ho ordinato questo

NON O OR-DEE-Nah-TO
KWAS-TO

Is the bill correct?

Il conto è esatto?

EL KON-TO A A-Zah'T-TO

Bring me...

Per favore, mi porti...

PER Fah-VO-RA MEE POR-TEE...

another spoon

un altro cucchiaio

OON ahL-TRO KOOK-Yah-YO

another fork

un' altra forchetta

OON ahL-TRah FOR-KAT-Tah

another plate please

un altro piatto

OON ahL-TRO PEE-ah'T-TO

GETTING AROUND

Getting around in a foreign country can be an adventure in itself! Taxi and bus drivers do  not always speak English, so it is essential to be able to give simple directions. The words and phrases in this chapter will help you get where you're going.

- Trains are used frequently by visitors to Europe. Schedules and timetables are easily understood. Arrive early to allow time for ticket purchasing and checking in and remember, trains leave on time!

- Metropoitana or subway is an inexpensive underground train system in Italy. M signifies a metro stop!

- Check with your travel agent about special rail passes which allow unlimited travel within a set period of time.

SIGNS TO LOOK FOR:

BIGLIETTERIA (TICKET OFFICE)

TAXI

TREN (TRAIN)

KEY WORDS

Airport (See page 82)

Aeroporto

@-Ⓐ-ℝⓄ-PⓄℝ-TⓄ

Bus Station / Bus Stop (See page 84)

Stazione degli autobus
Fermata dell' autobus

STⓐ-TSⒺ-Ⓞ-NⒶ DⒶ-LⒺ Ⓞⓦ-TⓄ-BⓄⓄS

FⒺℝ-Mⓐ-Tⓐ DⒺL Ⓞⓦ-TⓄ-BⓄⓄS

Car Rental Agency (See page 86)

Agenzia di autonoleggio

@-JⒺN-TSⒺ-Yⓐ DⒺ

Ⓞⓦ-TⓄ-NⓄ-LⒶ-CHⓄ

Subway Station (See page 88)

Metropolitana

MⒶ-Tℝ Ⓞ-PⓄ-LⒺ-Tⓐ-Nⓐ

Taxi Stand (See page 90)

Posteggio dei taxi

PⓄ-STⒶ-JⓄ DⒶ Tⓐ K-SⒺ

Train Station (See page 88)

Stazione dei treni

STⓐ-TSⒺ-Ⓞ-Nⓐ DⒶ Tℝ Ⓔ-NⒺ

AIR TRAVEL

Arrivals
Arrivi
ah-REE-VEE

Departures
Partenze
PahR-TĕN-TSA

Flight number...
Numero di volo...
NŌŌ-MA-RŌ DEE VŌ-LŌ...

Airline
Compagnia aerea
KŌM-Pah-NEE-ah ah-ĕ-RA-ah

The gate
Il cancello
EEL Kah-N-CHĕL-LŌ

Information
Informazione
EEN-FŌR-Mah-TSEE-Ō-NA

Ticket (airline)
Biglietto aereo
BEEL-YA'T-TŌ ah-ĕ-RA-Ō

Reservations
Prenotazioni
PRA-NŌ-Tah-TSEE-Ō-NEE

Note: See arrival section for phrases on baggage

I would like a seat...

Vorrei un posto...

↓ VO-RA' ON POS-TO...

in the no smoking section

Tra i non fumatori

TRah EE NON FOO-Mah-TO-REE

next to the window

Accanto al finestrino

ahK-Kah'N-TO ahL FEE-NeS-TREE'-NO

on the aisle

Vicino al corridoio

VEE-CHEE'-NO ahL KO-REE-DO'-EE-O

near the exit

Vicino all' uscita

VEE-CHEE'-NO ahL LOO-SHEE'-Tah

in first class

in prima classe

EEN PREE'-Mah KLah'S-SA

THE BUS

Bus

Autobus

ⓄⓌ-TⓄ-BⓄⓄS

Where is the bus stop?

Dov'è la fermata dell' autobus?

DⓄ-VⒺ́ LⓐH FⒺR-Mⓐ́-Tⓐ
DⒺL LⓄⓌ-TⓄ-BⓄⓄS

Do you go to...?

Va a...?

Vⓐ ⓐ...

What is the fare?

Quanto costa il biglietto?

KWⓐN-TⓄ KⓄ́S-Tⓐ ⒺL BⒺⒺL-YⒶ́-TⓄ

Where can I buy a bus ticket?

Dove vendono i biglietti dell' autobus?

DⓄ́-VⒶ VⒺN-DⓄ́-NⓄ ⒺⒺ
BⒺⒺL-YⒺ́T-TⒺⒺ DⒺL LⓄⓌ-TⓄ-BⓄⓄS

How often do the buses run?

Ogni quanti minuti passa l'autobus?

Ⓞ-NⒺⒺ KWⓐN-TⒺⒺ MⒺⒺ-NⓄⓄ-TⒺⒺ
Pⓐ́S-Sⓐ LⓄⓌ-TⓄ-BⓄⓄS

PHRASEMAKER

Please tell me...

Per favore mi dica...

PĕR Fah-VŌ-Rah MEE DEE-Kah...

which bus goes to...

quale autobus va a...

KWah-LA ow-TO-BooS Vah ah...

what time the bus leaves

a che ora parte l'autobus

ah KA Ō-Rah PahR-TA
Low-TO-BooS

where the bus stop is

Dov'è la fermata dell' autobus?

DO-Vĕ Lah FĕR-Mah-Tah
DĕL ow-TO-BooS

where to get off

quando devo scendere

KWah-N-DO DA-VO
SHĕN-DA-Rah

BY CAR

Fill it up

Faccia il pieno

F@-CH@ @L P@-@-N@

Please check...

Per piacere, controlli...

PPC K@N-TR@L-L@...

the oil

l'olio

L@-L@-@

the battery

la batteria

L@ B@T-T@-R@-@

the tires

le gomme

L@ G@M-M@

the water

l'acqua

L@-KW@

the brakes

i freni

@ FR@-N@

Can you help me?

Può aiutarmi?

PWO ah-YOO-TahR-MEE

My car won't start

La mia auto non parte

Lah MEE-ah ow-TO NON PahR-TA

I need a mechanic

Ho bisogno di un meccanico

O BEE-ZON-YO DEE
OON MAK-Kah-NEE-KO

Can you fix it?

Può aggiustarla?

PWO ah-JOOS-TahR-Lah

What will it cost?

Quanto mi costerà?

KWahN-TO MEE KOS-TA-Bah

How long will it take?

Quanto tempo ci vorrà?

KWahN-TO TēM-PO
CHEE VO-Bah

SUBWAYS AND TRAINS

Where is the subway station?

Dov'è la stazione della metropolitana?

DO-Vế Lah STah-TSEE-Ố-NA
DẾL-Lah MA-TRO-PO-LEE-Tah-Nah

Where is the train station?

Dov'è la stazione dei treni?

DO-Vế Lah STah-TSEE-Ố-NA
DA TRẾ-NEE

A one way ticket please

Un biglietto d' andata, per piacere

ooN BEEL-YAT-TO Dah N-Dah-Tah PPC

A round trip ticket

Un biglietto d' andata e ritorno

ooN BEEL-YẤ-TO DahN-Dah-Tah
ế REE-TOR-NO

First class

Prima classe

PREE-Mah KLah S-SA

Second class

Seconda classe

SA-KON-Dah KLah S-SA

Which train do I take to go to...

Quale treno devo prendere per andare a...

KWAH-LA TREH-NO DA-VO
PREN-DA-RA PER AHN-DAH-RA ah...

What is the fare?

Quanto costa il biglietto?

KWAHN-TO KOS-Tah
EL BEEL-YAT-TO

Is this seat taken?

Questo posto è occupato?

KWAS-TO POS-TO
A O-KOO-PAH-TO

Do I have to change trains?

Devo cambiare treno?

DA-VO KahM-BEE-ah-RA
TREH-NO

Does this train stop at...?

Questo treno ferma a...?

KWAS-TO TREH-NO
FER-Mah ah...

TAXI

Can you call a taxi for me?

Potrebbe chiamarmi un taxi?

PO-TRAB-BA KEE-ah-MAR-MEE

OON Tah'K-SEE

Are you available?

E' libero?

A LEE-BA-RO

I want to go...

Vorrei andare...

VO-RA' ahN-Dah-RA...

Stop here please

Si fermi qui per piacere

SEE FER-MEE KWEE PPC

Please wait

Mi aspetti per piacere

MEE ah-SPAT-TEE PPC

How much do I owe?

Quanto le devo?

KWahN-TO LA DA-VO

PHRASEMAKER

I would like to go...

Vorrei andare...

V①-B⒜ ⒜N-D⒜-B⒜...

to the hotel...

all' hotel...

⒜L ①-T⒠L...

to this address

a questo indirizzo

⒜ KW⒜S-T① ⒠N-D⒠-B⒠T-TS①

to the airport

all 'aeroporto

⒜L ⒜-Ⓐ-B①-P①B-T①

to the subway station

alla stazione della metropolitana

⒜-L⒜ ST⒜-TS⒠-①-N⒜ D⒠L-L⒜
M⒜-TB①-P①-L⒠-T⒜-N⒜

to the hospital

all' ospedale

⒜L ①S-P⒜-D⒜-L⒜

SHOPPING

Whether you plan a major shopping spree or just need to purchase some basic necessities, the following information is useful.

- Italy is rich in regional arts and crafts, and local shopkeepers entertain friendly bargaining with customers.

- Stores usually close between 1:00 p.m. and 4:00 p.m. in the afternoon. Some shops will be closed during the summer for vacation.

- Always keep receipts for everything you buy!

SIGNS TO LOOK FOR:

TABACCHERIA (SMOKE SHOP)

LIBRERIA (BOOKSTORE)

MAGAZZIINO (DEPARTMENT STORE)

CALZATURIFICIO (SHOE STORE)

GIOIELLERIA (JEWELRY SHOP)

SUPERMERCATO (SUPERMARKET)

FORNAIO (BAKERKY)

KEY WORDS

Credit card

Carta di credito

K(ah)R-T(ah)   D(EE)   KR(A)-D(EE)-T(O)

Money

Soldi /Denaro

S(O)L-D(EE) / D(A)-N(ah)-R(O)

Receipt

ricevuta

R(EE)-CH(A)-V(oo)-T(ah)

Sale

Vendita

V(A)N-D(EE)-T(ah)

Store

Negozio

N(A)-G(O)-TS(EE)-(O)

Travelers' checks

Travelers check

TR(ah)-V(e)-L(e)RS CH(e)K

USEFUL PHRASES

Do you sell...?

Vende...?

VⓔN-Dⓐ...

Do you have...?

Avete...?

ⓐⓗ-Vⓐ-Tⓐ...

I want to buy...

Vorrei comprare...

VⓄ-R-Ⓐ KⓄM-PRⓐⓗ-RⒶ...

How much?

Quanto costa?

KWⓐⓗN-TⓄ KⓄS-Tⓐⓗ

When are the shops open?

Qual'è l'orario dei negozi?

KWⓐⓗ-LⒶ LⓄ-Rⓐⓗ-RⒺⒺ-Ⓞ DⒶ NⒶ-GⓄ-TSⒺⒺ

No thank you

No, grazie

NⓄ GRⓐⓗ-TSⒺⒺ-Ⓐ

I´m just looking

Sto solo guardando

STⓄ SⓄ-LⓄ GWⓐⓗR-DⓐⓗN-DⓄ

It's very expensive

E' Molto costoso

Ⓐ MÓL-TⓄ KⓄS-TÓ-ZⓄ

Can't you give me a discount?

Potrebbe farmi uno sconto?

PⓄ-TRⒶB-BⒶ FⓐⓇ-MⒺ
ⓄⓄ-NⓄ SKⓄN-TⓄ

I'll take it!

Lo prendo!

LⓄ PRⒺN-DⓄ

I'd like a receipt please

Vorrei la ricevuta, per piacere

VⓄ-RⒶ Lⓐ RⒺ-CHⒶ-VⓄⓄ-Tⓐ PPC

I want to return this

Vorrei restituire questo

VⓄ-RⒶ RⒺS-TⒺ-TⓄⓄ-Ⓔ-RⒶ
KWⒶS-TⓄ

It doesn't fit

Non è la mia misura

NⓄN Ⓐ Lⓐ MⒺ-ⓐ
MⒺ-SⓄⓄ-Rⓐ

PHRASEMAKER

I'm looking for...

Sto cercando...

STO CHĕR-KahN-DO...

a bakery

una panetteria

OO-Nah Pah-NAT-Tĕ-REE-ah

a bank

una banca

OO-Nah BahN-Kah

a barber shop

un barbiere

OO-Nah BahR-BEE-A-RA

a book store

una libreria

OO-Nah LEE-BRA-REE-ah

a camera shop

un negozio di macchine fotografiche

OON NA-GO-TSEE-O DEE
MahK-KEE-NA FO-TO-GRah-FEE-KA

a florist shop

un fiorista

@N FEE-@-REES-T@h

a hair salon

un parrucchiere

@N P@h-R@K-KEE-@-R@

a pharmacy

una farmacia

@-N@h F@hR-M@h-CHEE-@h

Do you sell...

Vende...

↓ VeeN-D@...

aspirin?

aspirina?

@hS-PEE-REE-N@h

cigarettes?

sigarette?

SEE-G@h-R@T-T@

dresses?

abiti da donna?

@h-BEE-TEE

↓ D@h D@N-N@h

shirts?

camicie?

K@h-MEE-CH@

deodorant?
deodorante?

D@-Ⓞ-DⓄ-Rⓐ́N-T@

film?
rullini fotografici?

RⓞⓞL-LⒺ́-NⒺ
FⓄ-TⓄ-GRⓐ-FⒺ́-CHⒺ

pantyhose?
collant?

KÓ́L-Lⓐ́NT

perfume?
profumo?

PRⓄ-Fⓞⓞ́-MⓄ

razor blades?
lamette?

Lⓐ-Mⓐ́T-T@

shaving cream?
crema da barba?

KRⓐ́-Mⓐ Dⓐ Bⓐ́R-Bⓐ

soap?
sapone

Sⓐ-PⓄ́-N@

shampoo?
Shampoo?

SHⓐ́M-PⓄ

sunglasses?

occhiali da sole?

OK-KEE-ah'-LEE Dah SO'-LA

sunscreen?

crema antisolare?

KRA'-Mah ahN-TEE-SO-Lah'-RA

toothbrushes?

spazzolino da denti?

SPah T-TSO-LEE'-NO DA DeN-TEE

toothpaste?

dentifricio?

DeN-TEE-FREE'-CHO

water? (bottled)

bottiglie d'acqua?

BOT-TEE'-GLEE-A Dah'-KWah

water? (mineral)

Acqua minerale

ah'-KWah MEE-NA-Rah'-LA

ESSENTIAL SERVICES

Placing phone calls, mailing postcards and exchanging money are a few tasks you may need to perform while traveling.

THE BANK

As a traveler in a foreign country your primary contact with banks will be to exchange money.

- Have your passport handy when changing money.

- Change enough funds before leaving home to pay for tips, food and transportation to your final destination.

- Generally, you will receive a better rate of exchange at a bank than at an exchange office or airport.

- Current exchange rates are posted in bank and published daily in city newspapers.

SIGNS TO LOOK FOR:

BANCA (BANK)

UFFICIO DI CAMBIO (EXCHANGE OFFICE)

KEY WORDS

Bank

Banca

B⒜́N-K⒜

Exchange office

Ufficio di cambio

⒪⒪-F⒠́-CH⒪ D⒠ K⒜́M-B⒠-⒪

Money

Soldi / Denaro

S⒪́L-D⒠ / D⒜-N⒜́-⒭⒪

Money order

Mandato di pagamento

M⒜N-D⒜́-T⒪ D⒠ P⒜-G⒜-M⒠́N-T⒪

Travelers checks

Travelers check

T⒭⒜́-V⒠-L⒠⒭S CH⒠K

Currency

Lira   Lire (plural)

L⒠́-⒭⒜   L⒠́-⒭⒜

(Main unit of currency)

USEFUL PHRASES

Where is the bank?

Dov'è la banca?

DO-Vễ Lah Bah́N-Kah

What time does the bank open?

A che ore apre la banca?

ah KA O´-RA ah́-PRA Lah Bah́N-Kah

Where is the exchange office?

Dov'è l'ufficio di cambio?

DO-Vễ Loo-Fễ-CHO
Dễ Kah́M-Bễ-O

What time does the exchange office open?

A che ora apre l'ufficio di cambio?

ah KA O´-Rah ah́-PRA
Loo-Fễ-CHO Dễ Kah́M-Bễ-O

Can I change dollars here?

Posso cambiare i dollari qui?

PO´S-SO Kah́M-Bễ-ah́-RA ễ
DO´L-Lah-Rễ KWễ

Can you change this?

Puo' cambiarmi questo?

PW⊙ K⒜M-B⒠-⒜R-M⒠ KW⒜S-T⊙

What is the exchange rate?

Qual'è il cambio?

KW⒜-L⒜ ⒠L K⒜M-B⒠-⊙

I would like large bills

Vorrei banconote di grosso taglio

V⊙-R⒜ B⒜N-K⊙-N⊙-T⒜ D⒠ GR⊙S-S⊙ T⒜L-Y⊙

I would like small bills

Vorrei banconote di piccolo taglio

V⊙-R⒜ B⒜N-K⊙-N⊙-T⒜ D⒠ P⒠K-K⊙-L⊙ T⒜L-Y⊙

I need change

Ho bisogno di moneta spicciola

⊙ B⒠-Z⊙N-Y⊙ D⒠ M⊙-N⒜-T⒜ SP⒠-CH⊙-L⒜

Do you have an ATM?

Avete un bancomat?

⒜-V⒜-T⒜ ⊙⊙N B⒜N-K⊙-M⒜T

POST OFFICE

If you are planning on sending letters and postcards, be sure to send them early so that you don't arrive home before they do. **PT** or **POSTE E TELECOMUNICAZIONI** identifies the post office.

KEY WORDS

Air mail
Via aerea

VEE-ah ah-e-REE-ah

Letter
Una lettera

OO-Nah LET-TA-Rah

Post office
Ufficio postale

OOF-FEE-CHO POS-Tah-LA

Postcard
Cartolina postale

KahR-TO-LEE-Nah POS-Tah-LA

Stamp
Francobollo

FRahN-KO-BOL-LO

USEFUL PHRASES

Where is the post office?

Dov'è l'ufficio postale?

D◉-Vě L◉◉-Fℰℰ-CH◉ P◉S-T⒜ℎ-L⒜

What time does the post office open?

A che ore apre l'ufficio postale?

⒜ℎ K⒜ Ó-Ṟ⒜ ⒜ℎ-PṞ⒜
L◉◉-Fℰℰ-CH◉ P◉S-T⒜ℎ-L⒜

I need...

Ho bisogno di...

◉ Bℰℰ-Zó'N-Y◉ Dℰℰ...

stamps

francobolli

FṞ⒜N-K◉-Bó'L-Lℰℰ

an envelope

una busta

◉◉-N⒜ℎ B◉◉S-T⒜ℎ

a pen

una penna

◉◉-N⒜ℎ Pě'N-N⒜ℎ

TELEPHONE

Placing phone calls in a foreign country can be a test of will and stamina! Besides the obvious language barriers, service can vary greatly from one town to the next.

- If you have a choice do not call from your hotel room. Service charges can add a hefty amount to your bill.

- In Italy, phone calls can be made from public pay phones located in cafes and bars.

- You can place phone calls at telephone centers and pay for the call after completion.

- For AT&T USA direct, which allows you to be instantly connected to an operator in the U.S., dial 172 + 10 + 11.

SIGNS TO LOOK FOR:

TELEHONO (TELEPHONE)

TELEFONO PUBBLICO (PUBLIC TELEPHONE)

KEY WORDS

Telephone

Telefono

T@-L@-F①-N①

Information

Informazione

⑉N-F①R-M@-TS⑉-①-N@

Long distance

Internazionale

⑉N-T⑀R-N@-TS⑉-①-N@-L@

Operator

Signorina / Centralino

S⑉N-Y①-R⑉-N@ /
CH@N-TR@-L⑉-N①

Phone book

Guida telefonica

GW⑉-D@ T@-L@-F①-N⑉-K@

Public telephone

Telefono pubblico

T@-L@-F①-N① P⑳B-BL⑉-K①

USEFUL PHRASES

May I use your telephone?

Posso usare il suo telefono?

POS-SO oo-Zah-RA
EL Soo-O TA-LA-FO-NO

I don't speak Italian

Non parlo l'Italiano

NON PahR-LO LEE-Tah-LEE-ah-NO

I want to call (this number)...

Vorrei chiamare questo numero...

↓VO-RA KEE-ah-Mah-RA
↓KWAS-TO Noo-MA-RO

1 uno oo-NO		**2** due Doo-A	
3 tre TRA		**4** quattro KWah T-TRO	
5 cinque CHEEN-KWA		**6** sei SA-EE	
7 sette SAT-TA		**8** otto OT-TO	
9 nove NO-VA		**0** zero TSA-RO	

PHRASEMAKER

I would like to make a call...

Vorrei fare una telefonata...

V◎-R@́ F@́-R@ ◎◎́-N@

↓ T@-L@-F◎-N@́-T@...

long distance

Internazionale

€N-T€R-N@-TS€-◎-N@́-L@

collect

a carico del destinatario

@ K@́-R€-K◎

D€L D€S-T€-N@-T@́-R€-◎

person to person

diretta con preavviso

D€-R@́T-T@ K◎N

PR@-@V-V€́-Z◎

to the United States

negli stati uniti

N€́L-Y€ ST@́-T€ ◎◎-N€́-T€

SIGHTSEEING AND ENTERTAINMENT

In most towns in Italy you will find tourist information offices. Here you can usually obtain brochures, maps, historical information, bus and train schedules.

CITIES IN ITALY:

Roma (Rome)
RŌ-Mah

Napoli (Naples)
Nah-PŌ-LEE

Milano
MEE-Lah-NO

Pisa
PEE-Sah

Venezia (Venice)
VA-NA-TSEE-ah

Firenze (Florence)
FEE-RěN-TSA

KEY WORDS
Admission

Ingresso

ⒺN-GⓇⓔ´S-Sⓞ

Map

Cartina

Kⓐⓡ-TⒺ´-Nⓐⓗ

Reservation

Prenotazione

PⓇⒶ-NⓄ-Tⓐⓗ-TSⒺ-Ⓞ´-NⒶ

Ticket

Biglietto

BⒺL-YⒶ´T-Tⓞ

Tour

Viaggio / Gita

VⒺ-ⓐⓗ´-Jⓞ / JⒺ´-Tⓐⓗ

Tour guide

Guida turistica

GWⒺ´-Dⓐⓗ Tⓞⓞ-RⒺⒺ´S-TⒺ-Kⓐⓗ

USEFUL PHRASES

Where is the tourist office?

Dov'è l'ufficio del turismo?

DŌ-Vĕ́ LOO-FĒĒ-CHŌ DĕL
TOO-RĒĒS-MŌ

Is there a tour to...?

Avete un giro turistico per...?

ah-VÁ-Tah OON JĒĒ-RŌ
TOO-RĒĒS-TĒĒ-KŌ PĕR...

Where do I buy a ticket?

Dove posso comprare un biglietto per...?

DŌ-Vah PṒS-SO KOM-PRah́-Rah
OON BĒĒL-Yah́-TŌ PĕR...

How much does the tour cost?

Quanto costa il giro turistico?

KWah́N-TŌ KṒS-Tah ĒĒL JĒĒ-RŌ
TOO-RĒĒS-TĒĒ-KŌ

How long does the tour take?

Quanto dura il giro turistico?

KWah́N-TŌ DOO-Rah ĒĒL JĒĒ-RŌ
TOO-RĒĒS-TĒĒ-KŌ

Does the guide speak English?

La guida parla inglese?

L@ GW㎳-D@ P@R-L@ ㎱N-GL@-Z@

Are children free?

I bambini pagano?

㎱ B@M-B㎳-N㎳ P@-G@-N◎

What time does the show start?

A che ora comincia lo spettacolo?

@ K@ ◎-R@ K◎-M㎳N-CH@
L◎ SP㎳T-T@-K◎-L◎

Do I need reservations?

E' necessaria la prenotazione?

@ N@-CH@-S@-R㎳-@ L@
PR@-N◎-T@-TS㎳-◎-N@

Where can we go dancing?

Dove si puo' andare a ballare?

D◎-V@ S㎳ PW◎ @N-D@-R@
@ B@L-L@-R@

Is there a minimum cover charge?

C'e un prezzo d'ingresso?

CH@ ◎◎N PR@T-TS◎
D㎳N-GR㎳S-S◎

PHRASEMAKER

May I invite you...

Posso invitarla..

↓ PŌ´S-SŌ ⒺN-VⒺE-TⓐR-Lⓐ...

---

to a concert?

a un concerto?

ⓐ ⓄⓄN KⓄN-CHⓔ´R-TⓄ

---

to dance?

a ballare?

ⓐ Bⓐl-lⓐ´-Rⓐ

---

to dinner?

a pranzo?

ⓐ PRⓐ´N-TSⓄ

---

to the movies?

al cinema?

ⓐL CHⒺE´-Nⓐ-Mⓐ

---

to the theater?

al teatro?

ⓐL Tⓐ-ⓐ´-TRⓄ

Where can I find...

Dove posso trovare...

DŌ-V④ PŌS-SŌ TRŌ-V⒜-R④...

a golf course?

un campo da golf?

⓪N K⒜M-PŌ D⒜ GŌLF

a health club?

un club sportivo?

⓪N KL⓪B SPOR-T㊎-VŌ

a swimming pool?

una piscina?

⓪-N⒜ P㊎-SH㊎-N⒜

a tennis court?

un campo da tennis?

⓪N K⒜M-PŌ D⒜ T㊎N-N㊎S

HEALTH

Hopefully you will not need medical attention on your trip. If you do, it is important to communicate basic information regarding your condition.

- Check with your insurance company before leaving home to find out if you are covered in a foreign country.

- Have your prescriptions translated before you leave home.

- Take a small first aid kit with you. Include Band Aids, aspirin, cough syrup, throat lozenges, and vitamins.

- Your Embassy or Consulate should be able to assist you in finding health care.

- A closed pharmacy will post a notice on the door indicating the nearest open pharmacy.

SIGNS TO LOOK FOR:

OSPEDALE (HOSPITAL)

FARMACIA (PHARMACY)

KEY WORDS

Ambulance
Ambulanza

@M-B@-L@N-TS@

Dentist
Dentista

D@N-T@S-T@

Doctor
Medico

M@-D@-K@

Emergency!
Emergenza!

@-M@B-J@N-TS@

Hospital
Ospedale

@S-P@-D@-L@

Prescription
Ricetta

R@-CH@T-T@

USEFUL PHRASES

I am sick

Sono ammalato

SO-NO ah M-Mah-Lah-TO

I need a doctor

Ho bisogno di un dottore

O BEE-ZON-YO DEE
ON DOT-TO-Rah

It's an emergency!

E' un'emergenza!

A ON e-MeR-JeN-TSah

Where is the nearest hospital?

Dov'è l'ospedale più vicino?

DO-Ve LOS-PA-Dah-LA
PEE-oo VEE-CHEE-NO

Call an ambulance!

Chiamate un' ambulanza!

KEE-ah-Mah-TA
ON ah M-Boo-Lah N-TSah

I'm allergic to...

Sono allergico a...

SŌ-NŌ ahL-LĕR-JEE-KŌ ah...

I'm pregnant

Sono incinta

SŌ-NŌ EEN-CHĕN-Tah

I'm diabetic

Sono diabetico (male)
Sono diabetica (female)

SŌ-NŌ DEE-ah-Bĕ-TEE-KŌ
SŌ-NŌ DEE-ah-Bĕ-TEE-Kah

I have a heart condition

Sono debole di cuore

SŌ-NŌ DĀ-BŌ-Lah DEE KWŌ-Rah

I have high blood pressure

Ho la pressione alta

Ō Lah PRahS-SEE-Ō-Nah ahL-Tah

I have low blood pressure

Ho la pressione bassa

Ō Lah PRahS-SEE-Ō-Nah Bah́S-Sah

PHRASEMAKER

I need...

Ho bisogno di...

a doctor

un medico

ⓞN MⒶ-DⒺⒺ-KⓄ

a dentist

un dentista

ⓞN DⒺN-TⒺⒺ-S-Tⓐh

a nurse

un' infermiera

ⓞN ⒺⒺN-FⒺR-MⒺⒺ-Ⓐ-Rⓐh

an optician

un ottico

ⓞN ⓄT-TⒺⒺ-KⓄ

a pharmacist

un farmacista

ⓞN Fⓐh-R-Mⓐh-CHⒺⒺ-S-Tⓐh

(AT THE PHARMACY)

Do you have...?

Avete...?

ⓐⓗ-Vⓐ́-Tⓐ...

aspirin?

aspirina?

ⓐⓗS-Pⓔⓔ-Rⓔⓔ́-Nⓐⓗ

band aids?

cerotti?

CHⓔ̃-Rⓞ́T-Tⓔⓔ

cough medicine?

sciroppo per la tosse?

CHⓔⓔ-Rⓞ́P-Pⓞ Pⓔ̃R Lⓐⓗ Tⓞ́S-Sⓐ

ear drops?

gocce per le orecchie?

Gⓞ́-CHⓐ Pⓔ̃R Lⓐ ⓞ-Rⓐ́-KYⓐ

eye drops?

collirio?

KⓞL-Lⓔⓔ́-Rⓔⓔ-ⓞ

PHRASES FOR BUSINESS TRAVELERS

It is important to show appreciation and interest in another person's language and culture, particularly when doing business. A few well pronounced phrases can make a great impression.

KEY WORDS

Appointment

Appuntamento

ahP-POON-Tah-MĕN-TO

Meeting

Incontro

EEN-KON-TRO

Marketing

Marketing

MahR-Kĕ-TEEN

Presentation

Presentazione

PRĕ-ZĕN-Tah-TSEE-O-NA

Sales

Vendite

VAN-DEE-TA

USEFUL PHRASES

I have an appointment

Ho un appuntamento

Ⓞ ⓄⓄN ⓐhP-PⓄⓄN-Tⓐh-Mⓔ̆N-TⓄ

Here is my card

Ecco il mio biglietto da visita

Ⓔ̆K-KⓄ ⒺⒺL MⒺⒺ-Ⓞ BⒺⒺL-YⒶ-TⓄ
Dⓐh VⒺⒺ-ZⒺⒺ-Tⓐh

Can we get an interpreter?

Possiamo avere un interprete?

PⓄS-SⒺⒺ-ⓐh-MⓄ ⓐh-VⒶ-RⒶ
ⓄⓄN ⒺⒺN-Tⓔ̆R-PRⒶ-TⒶ

May I speak to Mr....?

Posso parlare con il signor...?

PⓄS-SⓄ PⓐhR-Lⓐh-RⒶ KⓄN
ⒺⒺL SⒺⒺN-YⓄR...

May I speak to Mrs...?

Posso parlare con la signora...?

PⓄS-SⓄ PⓐhR-Lⓐh-RⒶ KⓄN
Lⓐh SⒺⒺN-YⓄ-Rⓐh...

PHRASEMAKER

I need...

Ho bisogno di...

↓ Ⓞ BⒺⒺ-Z**Ó**N-YⓄ DⒺⒺ...

a computer
un computer

ⓄⓄN KⓄM-PY**Ó**Ⓞ-TⓔR

a copy machine
una fotocopiatrice

ⓄⓄ-Nⓐⓗ FⓄ-TⓄ-KⓄ-PⒺⒺ-ⓐⓗ-TRⒺⒺ-CHⒶ

a conference room
una sala conferenze

ⓄⓄ-Nⓐⓗ Sⓐⓗ-Lⓐⓗ KⓄN-FⓔⒺ-Rⓔ**Ⓔ**N-TSⒶ

a fax machine
una macchina per fax

ⓄⓄ-Nⓐⓗ Mⓐⓗ**K**-KⒺⒺ-Nⓐⓗ PⓔR FⓐⓗKS

an interpreter
un interprete

ⓄⓄN ⒺⒺN-TⓔR-PRⒶ-TⒶ

a lawyer
un avvocato

↓ ⓄⓄN ⓐⓗV-VⓄ-Kⓐⓗ-TⓄ

a notary

un notaio

ⓞⓞN Nⓞ-Tⓐⓗ-Yⓞ

overnight delivery

un recapito urgente

ⓞⓞN Rⓔ-Kⓐⓗ-Pⓔⓔ-Tⓞ ⓞⓞR-Jⓔ́N-Tⓐ

paper

di carta igienica

Dⓔⓔ Kⓐⓗ́R-Tⓐⓗ ⓔⓔ-Jⓐ́-Nⓔⓔ-Kⓐⓗ

a pen

una penna

ⓞⓞ́-Nⓐⓗ Pⓔ́N-Nⓐⓗ

a pencil

una matita

ⓞⓞ́-Nⓐⓗ Mⓐⓗ-Tⓔⓔ́-Tⓐⓗ

a secretary

una segretaria

ⓞⓞ́-Nⓐⓗ Sⓔ́G-Rⓔ-Tⓐⓗ́R-Yⓐⓗ

GENERAL INFORMATION

THE DAYS

Monday	**Tuesday**
Lunedí	Martedí
LOO-NA-DEE′	MAH-TĔ-DEE′
Wednesday	**Thursday**
Mercoledí	Giovedí
MĔR-KO-LA-DEE′	JO-VA-DEE′
Friday	**Saturday**
Venerdí	Sabato
VA-NĔR-DEE′	SAH′-BAH-TO
Sunday	
Domenica	
DO-MA′-NEE-KAH	

THE MONTHS

January	**February**
Gennaio	Febbraio
JĔN-NAH′-YO	FĔB-BRAH′-YO
March	**April**
Marzo	Aprile
MAH′R-TSO	AH-PREE′-LA

May
Maggio

M(ah)-J(O)

June
Giugno

J(oo)N-Y(O)

July
Luglio

L(oo)L-Y(O)

August
Agosto

(ah)-G(O)S-T(O)

September
Settembre

S(e)T-T(e)M-BR(A)

October
Ottobre

(O)T-T(O)-BR(A)

November
Novembre

N(O)-V(e)M-BR(A)

December
Dicembre

D(ee)-CH(e)M-BR(A)

THE SEASONS

Spring
Primavera

PR(EE)-M(ah)-V(e)-R(ah)

Summer
Estate

(e)S-T(ah)-T(A)

Autumn
Autunno

(OW)-T(oo)N-N(O)

Winter
Inverno

(EE)N-V(e)R-N(O)

NUMBERS

0	**1**	**2**
zero	uno	due
TSÁ-RO	OO'-NO	DOO'-A

3	**4**	**5**
tre	quattro	cinque
TRA	KWah'T-TRO	CHEEN-KWA

6	**7**	**8**
sei	sette	otto
SA	SAT'-TA	OT'-TO

9	**10**	**11**
nove	dieci	undici
NO'-VA	DEE-ê'-CHEE	OON-DEE-CHEE

12	**13**
dodici	tredici
DO'-DEE-CHEE	TRA'-DEE-CHEE

14	**15**
quattordici	quindici
KWah'T-TOR-DEE-CHEE	KWEEN-DEE-CHEE

16	**17**
sedici	diciassette
SA-DEE-CHEE	DEE-CHahS-Sê'T-TA

18

diciotto

DEE-CHOT-TO

19

diciannove

DEE-CHahN-NO-VA

20

venti

VAN-TEE

30

trenta

TRAN-Tah

40

quaranta

KWah-RahN-Tah

50

cinquanta

CHEEN-KWahN-Tah

100

cento

CHEN-TO

1000

mille

MEEL-LA

1,000,000

milione

MEEL-YO-NA

COLORS

Black

Nero

NÃ-RO

Blue

Blu

BLOO

Brown

Marrone

Mah-RO-NÃ

Gold

Oro

O-RO

Gray

Grigio

GREE-JO

Green

Verde

VÊR-DÃ

Orange

Arancione

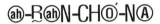 ⓐⓗ-ⓇⓐⓗN-CHⓄ-Nⓐ

Pink

Rosa

ⓇⓄ-Sⓐⓗ

Purple

Porpora

PⓄR-PⓄ-Ⓡⓐⓗ

Red

Rosso

ⓇⓄS-SⓄ

White

Bianco

BⒺⒺ-ⓐⓗN-KⓄ

Yellow

Giallo

JⓐⓗL-LⓄ

DICTIONARY

Adjectives are shown in their masculine form, as common practice dictates.

Each English entry is followed by the Italian spelling and the EPLS spelling.

A

a, an un, uno OON / OO-NO

a lot molto MOL-TO

able (to be) potére PO-TE-RE

above sopra SO-PRah

accident incidente EEN-CHEE-DEN-TA

accommodation sistemazione SEES-TE-Mah-TSEE-O-NA

account conto KON-TO

address indirizzo EEN-DEE-REET-TSO

admission ingresso EEN-GRES-SO

afraid (to be) aver paura ah-VER Pah-oo-Rah

after dopo DO-PO

afternoon pomeriggio PO-MA-REE-JO

agency agenzia ah-JEN-TSEE-Yah

air conditioning aria condizionata
    ah-REE-ah KON-DEE-TSEE-O-Nah-Tah

aircraft aereo ah-E-RA-O

airline compagnia aerea KOM-Pah-NEE-ah ah-E-RA-ah

airport aeroporto ah-A-RO-POR-TO

aisle corridoio KO-REE-DO-EE-O

all tutto TOOT-TO

almost quasi KWah-ZEE

alone solo SO-LO

also anche ahN-KA

always sempre SEM-PRA

ambulance ambulanza ahM-Boo-LahN-TSah

American americano ah-MA-REE-Kah-NO

and e E

another un altro OON ahL-TRO

anything qualsiasi cosa KWahL-SEE-ah-SEE KO-Sah

apartment appartamento ahP-PahR-Tah-MEN-TO

appetizers antipasti ahN-TEE-PahS-TEE

apple mela MA-Lah

appointment appuntamento ahP-POON-Tah-MEN-TO

April aprile ah-PREE-LA

arrival arrivo ah-REE-VO

arrive (to) arrivare ah-REE-Vah-RA

ashtray portacenere POR-Tah-CHA-Nah-RA

aspirin aspirina ahS-PEE-REE-Nah

attention attenzione ahT-TEN-TSEE-O-NA

August agosto ah-GOS-TO

author autore ow-TO-RA

automobile macchina Mah-KEE-Nah

Autumn autunno ow-TOON-NO

avenue corso KOR-SO

awful terribile TER-REE-BEE-LAY

B

baby bambino Bah-M-BEE-NO

babysitter babysitter BA-BEE-SEE-TER

bacon pancetta PahN-CHAT-Tah

bad cattivo KahT-TEE-VO

bag borsa BOR-Sah

baggage bagaglio Bah-GahL-YO

baked al forno ahL FOR-NO

bakery fornaio FOR-Nah-EE-O

banana banana Bah-Nah-Nah

bandage benda BEN-Dah

bank banca BahN-Kah

barber shop barbiere BahB-BEE-A'-RA

bartender barista Bah-REES-Tah

bath bagno BahN-YO

bathing suit costume da bagno KOS-Too-MA Dah BahN-YO

bathroom bagno BahN-YO

battery batteria BahT-TA-REE-ah

beach spiaggia SPEE-ah'-Jah

beautiful bellissimo BEL-LEES-SEE-MO

beauty shop salone di belleza Sah-LO'-NA DEE BEL-LET-Sah

bed letto LET-TO

beef manzo MahN-TSO

beer birra BEE-Rah

bellman fattorino Fah-TO-REE-NO

belt cintura CHEEN-Too-Rah

big grande GRahN-DA

bill conto KON-TO

black nero NA'-RO

blanket coperta KO-PER-Tah

blue blu BLoo

boat barca BahB-Kah

book libro LEE-BRO

book store libreria LEE-BRA-REE-ah

border confine KON-FEE-NA

boy ragazzo Bah-GahT-TSO

bracelet bracciale BRah-CHEE-ah'-LA

brakes freni FRA'-NEE

bread pane Pah-NA

breakfast colazione KO-Lah-TSEE-O'-NA

broiled alla griglia AL-LAH GREL-YAH
brown marrone MAH-RO-NA
brush spazzola SPAHT-TSO-LAH
building edificio A-DEE-FEE-CHO
bus autobus OW-TO-BOOS
bus station stazione degli autobus STAH-TSEE-O-NA DAL-YEE OW-TO-BOOS
bus stop fermata dell' autobus FER-MAH-TAH DEL OW-TO-BOOS
business affari AHF-FAH-REE
butter burro BOO-RO
buy (to) comprare KOM-PRAH-RA

C
cab taxi TAHK-SEE
call (to) chiamare KEE-AH-MAH-RA
camera macchina fotografica MAH-KEE-NAH FO-TO-GRAH-FEE-KAH
candy caramella KAH-RAH-MAL-LAH
car auto AH-OO-TO
carrot carota KAH-RO-TAH
castle castello KAHS-TEL-LO
cathedral cattedrale KAH-TA-DRAH-LA
celebration celebrazione CHA-LA-BRAH-TSEE-O-NA
center centro CHEN-TRO
cereal cereali CHA-RA-AH-LEE
chair sedia SA-DEE-AH
champagne champagne SHAHM-PAHN-YAH
change (exact) resto RES-TO
change (to) cambiare KAHM-BEE-AH-RA
cheap a buon mercato AH BWON MER-KAH-TO
check (bill in a restaurant) conto KON-TO

cheers salute Sah-LOO-Tah

cheese formaggio FOR-Mah-JO

chicken pollo POL-LO

child bambino BahM-BEE-NO

chocolate (flavor) cioccolata CHOK-KO-Lah-Tah

church chiesa KEE-A-Sah

cigar sigaro SEE-Gah-RO

cigarettes sigarette SEE-Gah-RAT-TA

city citta CHEET-Tah

clean pulito POO-LEE-TO

close (to) chiudere KEE-OO-DA-RA

closed chiuso KEE-OO-ZO

clothes vestiti VaS-TEE-TEE

cocktail cocktail KOK-TaL

coffee caffé Kah-FA

cold (temperture) freddo FRaD-DO

comb pettine PaT-TEE-NA

come (to) venire VA-NEE-RA

company (business) ditta DaT-Tah

computer calcolatore Kah-KO-Lah-TO-RA

concert concerto KON-CHaR-TO

conference conferenza KON-Fa-RaN-TSah

conference room sala conferenze Sah-Lah
KON-Fa-RaN-TSA

congratulations congratulazioni
KON-GRah-TOO-Lah-TSEE-O-NEE

copy machine fotocopiatrice FO-TO-KO-PEE-ah-TREE-CHA

corn granturco GRahN-TOoR-KO

cough la tosse Lah TOS-SA

cover charge coperto KO-PaR-TO

crab granchi GRahN-KEE

cream crema KRA-Mah
credit card carta di credito KahR-Tah DE KRA-DE-TO
cup tazza Tah-TSah
customs dogana DO-Gah-Nah
D
dance (to) ballare Bah-L-Lah-RA
dangerous pericoloso PE-RE-KO-LO-SO
date (calendar) data Dah-Tah
day giorno JE-OR-NO
December dicembre DE-CHEM-BRA
delicious delizioso DE-LE-TSE-O-SO
delighted lietissimo LE-A-TE-SE-MO
dentist dentista DEN-TES-Tah
deodorant deodorante DA-O-DO-RahN-TA
department store grande magazzino GRahN-DA Mah-Gah-TSE-NO
departure partenza PahR-TEN-TSah
dessert dolce DOL-CHA
detour deviazione DE-VE-ah-TSE-O-NA
diabetic diabetico DE-ah-BE-TE-KO
diarrhea diarrea DE-ah-RA-ah
dictionary dizionario DE-TSE-O-Nah-RE-O
dinner cena CHA-Nah
dinning room sala da pranzo Sah-Lah Dah PRahN-TSO
directions indicazioni EN-DE-Kah-TSE-O-NE
dirty sporco SPOR-KO
disabled invalido EN-Vah-LE-DO
discount sconto SKON-TO
distance distanza DES-TahN-TSah
doctor dottore DOT-TO-RA
document documento DO-Koo-MEN-TO

dollar dollaro DŌL-Lah-RO

down giù Joo

downtown in centro EEN CHEN-TRO

dress vestito VeS-TEE-TO

drink (to) bere BA-RA

drive (to) guidare GWEE-Dah-RA

drugstore farmacia Fah-R-Mah-CHEE-ah

dry cleaner lavanderia a secco Lah-Vah-N-DA-REE-ah ah SEK-KO

duck anitra ah-NEE-TRah

E

ear drops gocce per le orecchie GO-CHA PeR LA O-RA-KEE-A

ear orecchio O-RA-KEE-O

early presto PRES-TO

east est eST

easy facile Fah-CHEE-LA

eat(to) mangiare Mah-N-Jah-RA

eggs (fried) uova fritte WO-Vah FREET-TA

eggs (scrambled) uova strapazzate WO-Vah STRah-Pah-TSah-TA

egg uovo WO-VO

electricity elettricità A-LAT-TREE-CHEE-Tah

elevator ascensore ah-SHAN-SO-RA

embassy ambasciata ahM-Bah-SHah-Tah

emergency emergenza e-MeR-JeN-TSah

English inglese EEN-GLA-ZA

enough basta BahS-Tah

entrance ingresso EEN-GReS-SO

envelope busta BooS-Tah

evening sera Se-Rah

everything tutto T(oo)T-T(o)
excellent eccellente (e)-CH(ah)L-L(e)N-T(a)
excuse me mi scusi M(ee) SK(oo)-Z(ee)
exit uscita (oo)-SH(ee)-T(ah)
expensive caro K(ah)-R(o)
eye drops gocce per gli occhi G(o)-CH(a) P(e)R LY(ee)
(O)K-K(ee)
eyes occhi (O)K-K(ee)
F
face faccia F(ah)-CH(ah)
far lontano L(o)N-T(ah)-N(o)
fare (cost) costo K(o)S-T(o)
fast veloce V(e)-L(o)-CH(a)
fax machine macchina per fax
M(ah)K-K(ee)-N(ah) P(e)R (ee) F(ah)KS
February febbraio F(e)B-BR(ah)-Y(o)
few alcuni (ah)L-K(oo)-N(ee)
film (for a camera) rullino R(oo)L-L(ee)-N(o)
fine (very well) bene B(a)-N(a)
finger dito D(ee)-T(o)
fingernail unghia (oo)N-G(ee)-(ah)
fire extinguisher estintore (e)S-T(ee)N-T(o)-R(a)
fire fuoco FW(o)-K(o)
first primo PR(ee)-M(o)
fish pesce P(a)-SH(a)
fit (to) andare bene (ah)N-D(ah)-R(a) B(a)-N(a)
flight volo V(o)-L(o)
floor (story) piano P(ee)-(ah)-N(o)
florist shop fiorista F(ee)-(o)-R(ee)S-T(ah)
flower fiore F(ee)-(o)-R(a)
food cibo CH(ee)-B(o)

foot piede PEE-A-DA

fork forchetta FOR-KAT-Tah

french fries patatine fritte Pah-Tah-TEE-NA FREET-TA

fresh fresco FRES-KO

Friday venerdi VA-NER-DEE

fried fritto FREET-TO

friend amico ahM-EE-KO

fruit frutta FROOT-Tah

funny divertente DEE-VER-TEN-TA

G

gas station distributore DEES-TREE-Boo-TO-RA

gasoline benzina BEN-TSEE-Nah

gate cancello KahN-CHEL-LO

gentleman signore SEN-YO-RA

gift regalo RE-Gah-LO

girl ragazza Rah-Gah-T-TSah

glass (drinking) bicchiere BEEK-YE-RA

glasses (eye) occhiali OK-KEE-ah-LEE

gloves guanti GWahN-TEE

go forza FOR-TSah

gold oro O-RO

golf course campo da golf KahM-PO Dah GOLF

golf golf GOLF

good buono BWO-NO

goodbye arrivederci ah-REE-VA-DER-CHEE

goose oca O-Kah

grapes uva OO-Vah

grateful grato GRah-TO

gray grigio GREE-JO

green verde VER-DA

grocery store drogheria DRO-GA-REE-ah

group gruppo GROOP-PO
guide guida GWEE-Dah

H

hair capelli Kah-PEL-LEE
hairbrush spazzola SPahT-TSO-Lah
haircut taglio di capelli TahL-YO DEE Kah-PEL-LEE
ham prosciutto PRO-SHOOT-TO
hamburger hamburger ahM-BOOR-GER
hand mano Mah-NO
happy felice / contento FE-LEE-CHah / KON-TEN-TO
have, I ho O
he lui LOO-EE
head testa TES-Tah
headache mal di testa MahL DEE TES-Tah
health club club sportivo KLOOB SPOR-TEE-VO
heart condition debole di cuore DA-BO-LA DEE KWO-RA
heart cuore KWO-RA
heat calore Kah-LO-RA
hello ciao CHow
help! aiuto ah-YOO-TO
here qui KWEE
holiday festa FES-Tah
hospital ospedale OS-PA-Dah-LA
hot dog hot dog ahT DahG
hotel hotel O-TEL
hour ora O-Rah
how come KO-Mah
hurry (to) sbrigarsi ZBREE-Gah-SEE

I

I io EE-O

ice cream gelato J®-L@h-T©

ice cubes cubetti di ghiaccio K©©-B@T-T® D® G®-@h-CH©

ice ghiaccio G®-@h-CH©

ill ammalato @hM-M@h-L@h-T©

important importante ®M-P©R-T@hN-T@

indigestion l'indigestione ®N-D®-J®S-T®-O-N@

information informazione ®N-F©R-M@h-TS®-O-N@

inn albergo @hL-B®R-G©

interpreter interprete ®N-T®R-PR@-T@

J

jacket giubbotto J©©-B©T-T©

jam marmellata M@hR-M@L-L@h-T@h

January gennaio J®N-N@h-Y©

jewelry gioielli J©-Y®L-L®

jewelry store gioielleria J©-Y®L-L@-R®-@h

job lavoro L@h-V©-R©

juice succo S©©K-K©

July luglio L©©L-Y©

June giugno J©©N-Y©

K

ketchup ketchup K®-CH©©P

key chiave K®-@h-V@

kiss bacio B@h-CH©

knife coltello K©L-T®L-L©

know, I sapere S@h-P@-R@

L

ladies (restroom) toilette per le donne TW@h-L®T P®R L@ D©N-N@

lady signora S®N-Y©-R@h

lamb agnello @hN-Y®L-L©

language lingua LEN-GWah
large grande GRahN-DA
late tardi TahR-DEE
laundry lavanderia Lah-VahN-DA-REE-ah
lawyer avvocato ahV-VO-Kah-TO
left (direction) sinistra SEE-NEES-TRah
leg gamba GahM-Bah
lemon limone LEE-MO-NA
less meno MA-NO
letter lettera LET-TA-Rah
lettuce insalata EEN-Sah-Lah-Tah
light luce LOO-CHA
like, I mi piace MEE PEE-ah-CHA
like, I would vorrei VO-RA-EE
lip labbro LahB-BRO
lipstick rossetto ROS-SAT-TO
little piccolo PEEK-KO-LO
live (to) vivere VEE-VA-RA
lobster aragosta ah-Rah-GOS-Tah
long lungo LOON-GO
lost perduto PER-DOO-TO
love amore ah-MO-RA
luck fortuna FOR-TOO-Nah
luggage bagaglio Bah-GahL-YO
lunch pranzo PRahN-TSO
M
maid cameriera Kah-MA-REE-A-Rah
mail posta POS-Tah
makeup trucco TROO-K-KO
man uomo WO-MO
manager direttore DEE-RAT-TO-RA

map cartina KaR-TEE-Nah
March marzo MahR-TSO
market mercato MeR-Kah-TO
matches fiammiferi FEE-ahM-MEE-FA-REE
May maggio Mah-JO
mayonnaise maionese Mah-YO-NA-SA
meal pasto Pah'S-TO
meat carne KahR-NA
mechanic meccanico MA-Kah-NEE-KO
medicine medicina MA-DEE-CHEE-Nah
meeting incontro EEN-KON-TRO
Mens (restroom) toilette per uomini TWah-LeT
   PeR WO-MEE-NEE
menu menù Me-Noo
message messaggio MAS-Sah-JO
milk latte Lah'T-TA
mineral water acqua minerale ah-KWah
   MEE-NA-Rah-LA
minute minuto MEE-Noo-TO
Miss signorina SeeN-YO-REE-Nah
mistake sbaglio SBah'L-YO
misunderstanding malinteso Mah-LEEN-TA-SO
moment momento MO-MeN-TO
Monday lunedi Loo-NA-DEE
money soldi SOL-DEE
month mese MA-SA
monument monumento MO-Noo-MeN-TO
more più PEE-oo
morning mattina Mah'T-TEE-Nah
mosque moschea MOS-KA-ah
mother madre Mah'-DRA

mountain montagna MON-TAN-Yah

movies film FEELM

Mr. signore SEEN-YO-RA

Mrs. signora SEEN-YO-Rah

much, too molto MOL-TO

museum museo Moo-SA-O

mushrooms funghi FooN-GEE

music musica Moo-SEE-Kah

mustard senape SA-Nah-PA

N

nail polish smalto per le unghie SMAL-TO
    PER LA ooN-GEE

name nome NO-MA

napkin tovagliolo TO-VAL-YO-LO

near vicino VEE-CHEE-NO

neck collo KOL-LO

need, I ho bisogno O BEE-ZON-YO ...

never mai MAH-EE

newspaper giornale JOR-NAH-LA

newstand edicola A-DEE-KO-Lah

next time la prossima volta Lah PROS-SEE-Mah VOL-Tah

night notte Lah NOT-TA

nightclub locale notturno LO-Kah-LA NOT-Too-R-NO

no no NO

no smoking non fumatori NON Foo-Mah-TO-REE

noon mezzogiorno MA-TSO-JOR-NO

north nord NORD

notary notaio NO-Tah-YO

November novembre NO-VEM-BRA

now adesso ah-DES-SO

number numero Noo-MA-RO

nurse infermiera EEN-FEER-MEE-A'-Rah

O

occupied occupato OK-Koo-Pah'-TO
ocean oceano O-CHA'-ah-NO
October ottobre OT-TO'-BRA
officer ufficiale EEL ooF-FEE-CHah'-LA
oil olio OL-YO
omelet frittata FREET-Tah'-Tah
one way (traffic) senso unico SEEN-SO oo-NEE-KO
onions cipolle CHEE-POL'-LA
open (to) aprire ah-PREE'-RA
opera opera O'-PA-Rah
operator centralinista CHEEN-TRah-LEE-NEE'S-Tah
optician ottico OT-TEE'-KO
orange (fruit) arancia ah-Rah'N-CHah
order (to) ordinare OR-DEE-Nah'-RA
original originale O-REE-JEE-Nah'-LA
owner proprietario PRO-PREE-A'-Tah-REE'-O
oysters ostriche O'S-TREE-KA

P

package pacco Pah'K-KO
paid pagato Pah-Gah'-TO
pain dolore DO-LO'-RA
painting dipinto DEE-PEEN-TO
pantyhose collant KOL-Lah'NT
paper carta Kah'R-Tah
park (to) parcheggiare Pah'R-KA-Jah'-RA
park parco Pah'R-KO
partner (business) socio SO'-CHO
party festa FEE'S-Tah
passenger passeggero Pah'S-SA-JEE'-RO

passport passaporto P@S-S@-P@R-T@

pasta pasta P@S-T@

pastry pasticceria P@S-T@-CH@-R@-@

pen penna P@N-N@

pencil matita M@-T@-T@

pepper pepe P@-P@

perfume profumo PR@-F@-M@

person persona P@R-S@-N@

person to person diretta con preavviso D@-R@T-T@
 K@N PR@-@-V@-Z@

pharmacist un farmacista @N F@R-M@-CH@S-T@

pharmacy farmacia F@R-M@-CH@-@

phone book elenco telefonico @-L@N-K@
 T@-L@-F@-N@-K@

photo foto F@-T@

photographer fotografo F@-T@-GR@-F@

pillow cuscino K@-SH@-N@

pink rosa R@-S@

pizza pizza P@T-S@

plastic plastica PL@S-T@-K@

plate piatto P@-@T-T@

please per favore / per piacere P@R F@-V@-R@ /
 P@R P@-@-CH@-R@

pleasure piacere P@-@-CH@-R@

police polizia P@-L@-TS@-@

police station stazione di polizia ST@-TS@-@-N@ D@
 P@-L@-TS@-@

pork maiale M@-Y@-L@

porter facchino F@-K@-N@

post office ufficio postale @-F@-CH@ P@S-T@-L@

postcard cartolina K@R-T@-L@-N@

potato patata P(ah)-T(ah)-T(ah)
pregnant incinta (ee)N-CH(ee)N-T(ah)
prescription ricetta R(ee)-CH(e)T-T(ah)
price prezzo PR(a)́-TS(o)
problem problema PR(o)-BL(a)́-M(ah)
profession professione PR(o)-F(e)S-S(ee)-(o)́-N(a)
public pubblico P(oo)B-BL(ee)-K(o)
public telephone telefono pubblico T(a)-L(a)́-F(o)-N(o)
    P(oo)B-BL(ee)-K(o)
puriified purificata P(oo)-R(ee)-F(ee)-K(ah)́-T(ah)
purple porpora P(o)́R-P(o)-R(ah)
purse borsetta B(o)R-S(a)́T-T(ah)
Q
quality qualitá KW(ah)-L(ee)-T(ah)́
question domanda D(o)-M(ah)́N-D(ah)
quickly in fretta (ee)N FR(a)́T-T(ah)
quiet (to be) zitto S(ee)T-T(o)
quiet! silenzio! S(ee)-L(e)́N-TS(ee)-(o)
R
radio radio R(ah)́-D(ee)-(o)
railroad ferrovia F(e)R-(o)-V(ee)́-(ah)
rain pioggia P(ee)-(o)́-J(ah)
raincoat impermeabile (ee)M-P(e)R-M(a)-(ah)́-B(ee)-L(a)
ramp rampa R(ah)́M-P(ah)
rare (steak) al sangue (ah)L S(ah)́N-GW(a)
razor blades lamette L(ah)-M(a)́T-T(a)
ready pronto PR(o)́N-T(o)
receipt ricevuta R(ee)-CH(a)-V(oo)́-T(ah)
recommend (to) raccomandare R(ah)K-K(o)-M(ah)N-D(ah)́-R(a)
red rosso R(o)́S-S(o)
repeat ripeta R(ee)-P(a)́-T(ah)

reservation prenotazione PRA-NO-Tah-TSEE-O'-NA

restaurant ristorante REES-TO-RahN-TA

return (to come back) ritornare REE-TOR-Nah-RA

return (to give back) restituire RES-TEE-Too-EE-RA

rice riso REE-ZO

rich ricco REK-KO

right (correct) giusto Joo'S-TO

right (direction) destra DE'S-TRah

road strada STRah-Dah

room stanza STahN-TSah

round trip andata e ritorno ahN-Dah-Tah E REE-TOR-NO

S

safe (box) cassaforte Kah-S-Sah-FOR-TA

salad insalata EEN-Sah-Lah'-Tah

sale vendita Vah'N-DEE-Tah

salmon salmone Sah-L-MON-A

salt sale Sah'-LA

sandwich panino Pah-NEE-NO

Saturday sabato Sah'-Bah-TO

scissors forbici FOR-BEE-CHEE

sculpture scultura SKoo-L-Too'-Rah

seafood pesce PA'-SHA

season stagione STah-JO'-NA

seat posto PO'S-TO

secretary segretario SEG-RE-Tah'R-YO

section sezione SE-TSEE-O'-NA

September settembre SET-TE'M-BRA

service servizio SER-VEE-TSEE-O

several diversi DEE-VER-SEE

shampoo shampoo SHahM-PO

sheets (on a bed) lenzuola LEN-TSWO-Lah

shirt camicia K@-MEE-CH@

shoe scarpa SK@R-P@

shoe store negozio di scarpe
    N@-GO-TSEE-O DEE SK@R-P@

shop (store) negozio N@-GO-TSEE-O

shopping center centro commerciale CHEN-TRO
    KO-MER-CHEE-@-L@

shower doccia DO-CH@

shrimp gamberetti G@M-B@-B@T-TEE

sick malato M@-L@-TO

sign (display) cartello K@R-TEL-LO

signature firma FEER-M@

single singolo SEEN-GO-LO

sir signore SEEN-YO-R@

sister sorella SO-REL-L@

size taglia T@L-Y@

skin pelle PEL-L@

skirt gonna GON-N@

sleeve manica M@N-NEE-K@

slowly lentamente LEN-T@-MEN-T@

small piccolo PEEK-KO-LO

smile (to) sorridere SOR-REE-D@-R@

smoke (to) fumare Foo-M@-R@

soap sapone S@-PON-@

sock calza K@L-TS@

some qualche KW@L-K@

something qualcosa KW@L-KO-Z@

sometimes a volte @ VOL-T@

soon presto PRES-TO

sorry (I am) mi dispiace MEE DEES-PEE-@-CH@

soup minestra MEE-N@S-TR@

south sud SooD
souvenir ricordo Ree-KOB-DO
Spanish spagnolo SPahN-YO-LO
speciality specialitá SPe-CHee-ah-Lee-Tah
speed velocitá VA-LO-CHee-Tah
spoon cucchiaio KooK-Yah-YO
sport sport SPOBT
Spring primavera Lah PBee-Mah-Ve-Bah
stairs scale SKah-LA
stamp francobollo FBahN-KO-BOL-LO
station stazione STah-TSee-O-NA
steak bistecca BeeS-TA-Kah
steamed al vapore ahL Vah-PO-BA
stop! Si fermi! See FeB-Mee
store negozio NA-GO-TSee-O
storm temporale TeM-PO-Bah-LA
straight ahead avanti diritto ah-VahN-Tee Dee-BeeT-TO
strawberry fragola FBah-GO-Lah
street via Vee-ah
string spago SPah-GO
subway metropolitana MA-TBO-PO-Lee-Tah-Nah
sugar zucchero TSooK-KA-BO
suit (clothes) abito completo ah-Bee-TO KOM-PLe-TO
suitcase valigia Vah-Lee-CHah
summer estate eS-Tah-TA
sun sole SO-LA
sun tan lotion crema solare KBA-Mah SO-Lah-BA
Sunday domenica DO-MA-Nee-Kah
sunglasses occhiali da sole OK-Kee-ah-Lee Dah SO-LA
supermarket supermercato Soo-PeB-MeB-Kah-TO
surprise sorpresa SOB-PBA-Zah

sweet dolce DOL-CHA
swim (to) nuotare NWO-Tah-RA
swimming pool piscina PEE-SHEE-Nah
synagogue sinagoga SEE-Nah-GO-Gah
T
table tavola Tah-VO-Lah
tampons tamponi TahM-PO-NEE
tape (sticky) nastro adesivo Nah'S-TRO ah-DE-SEE-VO
tape recorder registratore RE-JEE-STRah-TO-RA
tax imposta EEM-POS-Tah
taxi taxi Tah'K-SEE
tea té TA
telegram telegramma TA-LA-GRah'M-Mah
telephone telefono TA-LA-FO-NO
television televisione TA-LA-VEE-SEE-O-NA
temperature temperatura TEM-PER-ah-Too-Rah
temple tempio TEM-PEE-O
tennis court campo da tennis EEL Kah'M-PO Dah
    TEN-NEES
tennis tennis TEN-NEES
thank you molte grazie MOL-TA GRah-TSEE-A
that quello KWEL-LO
the il, la, lo, i, gli, le EEL/ Lah/ LO/ EE/ LYEE/ LA
theater teatro TA-ah-TRO
there la Lah
they loro LO-RO
this questo KWaS-TO
thread filo FEE-LO
throat gola GO-Lah
Thursday giovedi JO-VA-DEE
ticket biglietto BEE-LEE-A-TO

tie cravatta KRＡ-VＡT-TＡ

time ora Ｏ-RＡ

tip (gratuity) mancia MＡN-CHＡ

tire gomma GＯM-MＡ

tired stanco STＡN-KＯ

toast pane tostato PＡ-NＡ TＯS-TＡ-TＯ

tobacco tabacco TＡ-BＡK-KＯ

today oggi Ｏ-JＥ

toe dito del piede DＥ-TＯ DＥL PＥ-Ａ-DＡ

together insieme ＥN-SＥ-Ａ-MＡ

toilet paper carta igienica KＡR-TＡ Ｅ-JＡ-NＥ-KＡ

toilet toilette / gabinetto TWＡ-LＥT / GＡ-BＥ-NＡT-TＯ

tomato pomodoro PＯ-MＯ-DＯ-RＯ

tomorrow domani DＯ-MＡ-NＥ

tooth ache mal di denti MＡL DＥ DＥN-TＥ

toothbrush spazzolino da denti SPＡT-TSＯ-LＥ-NＯ DＡ DＥN-TＥ

toothpaste dentifricio DＥN-TＥ-FRＥ-CHＯ

toothpick stuzzicadenti STＯ-TSＥ-KＡ-DＥN-TＥ

tour giro JＥ-RＯ

tourist office ufficio del turismo Ｏ-FＥ-CHＯ DＥL TＯ-RＥS-MＯ

tourist turista TＯ-RＥS-TＡ

towel asciugamano Ａ-SHＯ-GＡ-MＡ-NＯ

train treno TRＡ-NＯ

travel agency agenzia di viaggio Ａ-JＥN-TSＥ-YＡ DＥ VＥ-Ａ-JＯ

travelers check travelers check TRＡ-VＥL-ＥRS CHＥKS

trip viaggio VＥ-Ａ-JＯ

trousers pantaloni PＡN-TＡ-LＯ-NＥ

trout veritá VＥ-RＥ-TＡ

truth verità Vé-REE-Tah
Tuesday martedí MahR-Té-DEE
turkey tacchino Tah-KEE-NO
U
umbrella ombrello OM-BRéL-LO
understand (to) capire Kah-PEE-Rah
underwear mutande Moo-TahN-DA
United States Stati Uniti STah-TEE oo-NEE-TEE
university universitá oo-NEE-VéR-SEE-Tah
up su Soo
urgent urgente ooR-JéN-TA
V
vacancies (accommodation) stanze libere
    STahN-TSA LEE-BA-RA
vacant libero LEE-BA-RO
vacation vacanza Vah-KahN-TSah
valuable di valore DEE Vah-LO-RA
value valore Vah-LO-RA
vanilla vaniglia Vah-NEEL-Yah
veal vitello VEE-TéL-LO
vegetables verdura VéR-Doo-Rah
view vista VEES-Tah
vinegar aceto ah-CHA-TO
voyage viaggio VEE-ah-JO
W
waiter cameriere Kah-MA-REE-A-RA
waitress cameriera Kah-MA-REE-A-Rah
want, I voglio VOL-YO
wash (to) lavare Lah-Vah-RA
watch orologio O-RO-LO-JO
watch out! attenzione! ahT-TéN-TSEE-O-NA

water acqua ah-KWah

watermelon anguria ahN-Goo-Ree-ah

we noi Noy

weather tempo TEM-PO

Wednesday mercoledí MER-KO-LA-DEE

week settimana SET-TEE-Mah-Nah

weekend fine settimana FEE-Nah SET-TEE-Mah-Nah

welcome benvenuto BEN-VE-Noo-TO

well done ben cotto BEN KO-TO

west ovest O-VEST

what? cosa? KO-Zah

wheelchair sedia a rotelle SAD-Yah ah RO-TEL-Lah

when? quando KWahN-DO

where dove DO-VA

which? quale KWah-Lah

white bianco BEE-ahN-KO

who chi KEE

why? perché PER-KA

wife moglie MOL-YA

wind vento VEN-TO

window finestra FEE-NES-TRah

wine list lista dei vini LES-Tah DA VEE-NEE

wine vino VEE-NO

winter inverno EEN-VER-NO

with con KON

woman donna DON-Nah

wonderful meraviglioso MA-Rah-VEEL-YO-SO

world mondo MON-DO

wrong (incorrect) sbagliato SBahL-Yah-TO

YZ

year anno ahN-NO

yellow giallo J@L-L©

yes sí S€€

yesterday ieri Y€-R€€

you tu T©©

zipper cerniera CH€R-N€€-@-R@

zoo zoo TS©-©

INDEX

CAN NOT FIND THESE OTHER
EASY TO PRONOUNCE
LANGUAGE PHRASE BOOKS ?
THEN RETURN THIS ORDER TO:

Griffin Publishing

Attn: Orders
544 W. COLORADO STREET
GLENDALE, CALIFORNIA 91204
818 244-2128

(Please Print)   Date:_____

Name:_____

Address:_____

City:_____ State:_____ Zip:_____

Phone:(_____)_____

Title	Price	Qty	Amount
ENGLISH TO SPANISH	$7.95	_____/_____	
ENGLISH TO ITALIAN	$7.95	_____/_____	
ENGLISH TO FRENCH	$7.95	_____/_____	
ENGLISH TO JAPANESE	$7.95	_____/_____	

Sub-Total:_____

8.25% Tax:_____

$2.00 1st Book add'l books $1.00 ea.   Shipping:_____

Total:_____

Payment Enclosed: **Made payable to Griffin Publishing**
    _____Check / Money Order   _____Visa / Master Card

Acc#_____

Exp. Date:_____

Signature:_____

Can't Wait Fax your Credit Card Orders to
(818) 242-1172